"I am not good with finance, but the concept of money boxes was introduced to me by Anand, and it made sense because it is very practical, easy to understand, and has helped me plan my finances so much better."

- **Ricken Desai,**
Professional Photographer

"This book is an eye-opener for managing and growing personal finance. The small and simple-to-follow tips ensure success in the long run."

– **Vidushi Author**
Writer, Friend

"Anand and I have been friends since our early teens, as we morphed into young men from little boys. It is now, in hindsight, after three decades of close association, that I understand well that his prowess with earning and, more importantly, managing money is no fluke - it was meant to be. An evolutionary process going through phases of growth with discipline and integrity. Integrity and honesty is his highest quality. His friendship is loyal, his business ethics are just and his work/life balance is in perfect equilibrium. His advice on matters of business and finances is straightforward and uncomplicated, which makes it easy to adopt, and with quick obvious results."

- **Shaji K**
Founder of South Aussie Marketing Co.,
Adelaide, Australia

MONEY
VIBE

*A fresh way to think about wealth
and success!*

ANAND MEHTA

STARDOM BOOKS

www.StardomBooks.com

STARDOM BOOKS
112 Bordeaux Ct.
Coppell, TX 75019, USA

FIRST EDITION MARCH 2025

STARDOM BOOKS, LLC.
112 Bordeaux Ct. Coppell, TX 75019, USA

www.stardombooks.com

Stardom Books, United States
Stardom Alliance, India

MONEY VIBE
A fresh way to think about wealth and success!

Anand Mehta

p. 190
cm. 13.97 X 21.59

Category: BUS050030 Business & Economics:
Personal Finance - Money Management
BUS027030 Business & Economics:
Finance - Wealth Management

ISBN: 978-1-957456-66-9

DEDICATION

To my wife, Vibha Anand Mehta
Whose unwavering love and endless patience illuminate my path,
And whose faith in me fuels every aspiration,
Inspiring me as I navigate this complex journey of life.

And to my father, Suresh Mehta
Whose wisdom, strength, and timeless lessons serve as my guide,
Leading me through the worlds of financial management and
purpose.

Your teachings resonate in the core of every page of this work.

This book is a heartfelt tribute to the noteworthy influence you
both have had on my life,
A reflection of the guidance and love that have shaped my jou

CONTENTS

ACKNOWLEDGMENTS

To my wife and son, who have been an inspiration, my parents, and my friends, specifically Khaja Shajiuddin.

To Amar Ohri, who kept telling me that my thoughts on money management are a true treasure trove of practical and insightful advice for understanding money.

To the Stardom Team, Raam Anand, who reached out to me asking me to write, and to the dedicated team of Ranjitha, Priyadarshini, Rekha, Chaya, Aakruti, and Harika.

A heartfelt thanks to all those who have been part of this journey. Your success stories achieved through my guidance have been a source of immense inspiration for this book. Witnessing the positive transformation in financial perceptions and mindsets among my friends and family has been deeply rewarding and motivated this effort.

This book is driven by a sincere goal: to empower more individuals in society with practical tools and insights for financial freedom.

Finally, I should not forget Sanjana Ghosh, who has been patient enough to listen to me throughout the journey and believed in me and my thought process about managing money. She has been very kind and is a wonderful person by nature.

"MONEY IS THE ONLY PAPER THAT GIVES YOU LOVE, POWER AND RESPECT."

₹1
NO MONEY?
KNOW MONEY!

FAQ

Q: Anand, why do you think so much before spending, even though you have so much?

It's not about overthinking each expense; it's about thinking of the bigger picture. When I spend, I don't dwell on the immediate satisfaction—my mind goes to the future. I ask myself, "If I spend now, will I regret this later? Could this money serve a more meaningful purpose down the line?" Every time we're about to spend, I think it's crucial to ask ourselves if it's truly necessary at that moment. Take, for example, the choice I made regarding my car—I carefully considered its necessity, rather than indulging on a whim.

"Don't become a philosopher before you are rich."

–Shah Rukh Khan, Celebrity

Imagine waking up every morning feeling confident about your financial future, knowing exactly where your money is going, and having a plan that lets you enjoy today while securing tomorrow. Sounds ideal, doesn't it? Yet, for many middle and upper-middle-class individuals, this financial security is often just a distant dream because of common money management pitfalls.

Managing money effectively isn't just about numbers; it's about laying the groundwork for a balanced and fulfilling life.

In this chapter, we'll explore the critical role of money management in achieving optimal life satisfaction and reducing stress. By understanding the importance of wisely handling your finances, you can take the first step toward financial confidence and lead a balanced and fulfilling life.

Money profoundly impacts various aspects of life, especially for middle and upper-middle-class individuals who often handle multiple financial responsibilities. Poor money management can lead to a cascade of negative outcomes, affecting health, relationships, and opportunities.

Financial stress can severely impact both physical and mental health. For instance, someone who hasn't managed their money well might face significant stress during emergencies, leading to conditions like hypertension, anxiety, and depression. Even research from the American Psychological Association (APA) highlights that financial stress is a significant source of chronic stress for many, leading to detrimental health effects over time.

One specific study[1] found that financial stress is associated with a 13% increase in the likelihood of experiencing a heart attack. This underscores the critical need for effective money management to mitigate health risks and promote overall well-being.

---

[1] "Significant Financial Stress Associated with 13-Fold Higher Odds of Having a Heart Attack," *Cardiovascular Journal of Africa* 29, no. 4 (2018): 217.

I have often seen money issues as a leading cause of conflicts in relationships. Whether it's borrowing or lending money among friends and family or disagreements about spending and saving habits, financial mismanagement can strain even the closest relationships. For example, disputes over unpaid loans can create rifts between friends and family members.

In my own experience and those around me, lending large sums of money to friends who fail to repay can seriously damage friendships. I've also noticed that money issues often lead to conflicts in marriages, with couples frequently arguing over spending priorities or debt management. If not addressed, these tensions can build and sometimes even lead to divorce.

Over time, I've learned that managing money well is key to seizing opportunities. Having some savings or a financial cushion makes it easier to take advantage of opportunities as they arise— whether it's investing in a new business, taking time off for education, or moving to a new city for a better job.

I've also noticed that middle and upper-middle-class individuals face unique financial challenges that can complicate effective money management. Despite decent incomes, high living expenses, debt, and the pursuit of a certain lifestyle can be obstacles.

Increasingly, lifestyle inflation emerges as one of the most common challenges, where increased income leads to proportionately higher spending. This prevents many from saving adequately and planning for the future. Despite earning a substantial income, many find themselves living paycheck to paycheck due to high living costs and the pressure to maintain a certain lifestyle.

Another challenge is managing complex financial obligations like mortgages, student loans, and credit card debt. The burden of these obligations can be overwhelming, leading to poor financial decisions and increased stress.

KNOW MONEY!

Poor money management can have several negative outcomes, including:

Financial Instability

Without effective money management, individuals may find themselves financially unstable and unable to handle unexpected expenses or emergencies. This often results in increased reliance on credit, which can worsen their financial troubles.

Reduced Quality of Life

Financial instability can also diminish the quality of life, as individuals might struggle to afford things they enjoy or invest in personal and professional growth opportunities. This can lead to feelings of frustration, disappointment, and decreased life satisfaction.

The Connection Between Good Money Management and Personal Happiness

From personal experiences, I've realized there is a strong connection between effective money management and personal happiness. Managing finances well can reduce stress, improve relationships, and open up opportunities for growth and fulfillment.

In fact, good financial management often revolves around key principles like budgeting, saving, and investing. Financial experts such as Dave Ramsey emphasize the importance of having a zero-based budget, where every dollar is allocated to a specific purpose. This method ensures that spending is intentional and aligned with one's financial goals, creating a sense of control and purpose.

I've seen firsthand how taking charge of finances can transform lives. For example, I once worked with a professional who was suffering from burnout due to financial stress. Together, we developed a comprehensive financial plan that focused on reducing debt, building savings, and regaining control over their financial future.

This plan not only helped them alleviate stress but also significantly improved their mental health and overall life satisfaction. It's clear that gaining control over your finances can lead to substantial improvements in various aspects of life.

Be Your Own Bank

"So this is my personal bank," I often tell people. "I don't just deposit money into banks; this is my bank." By managing money prudently—which means carefully planning for the future—individuals can create a personal safety net that provides security and peace of mind. This idea of being your own bank involves saving and investing wisely to ensure you have funds available for emergencies and opportunities without heavily relying on external financial institutions.

The link between financial health and overall well-being is well-documented. Numerous studies and statistics clearly demonstrate this impact. For example, the APA's annual 'Stress in America' survey[2] consistently shows that money is a top source of stress for professionals, affecting their health and relationships. According to the survey, 64% of respondents cited it as a very significant source of stress; this includes 77% of parents, 75% of Millennials (ages 18-35), and 76% of Gen Xers (ages 36-49).

According to a report[3] by the Consumer Financial Protection Bureau, individuals with higher financial well-being are more likely to feel secure about their financial future and less likely to experience financial stress. The report emphasizes that financial well-being involves more than just having money—it's about having control over your finances, the ability to absorb financial shocks, and the freedom to make choices that enhance your enjoyment of life. *(Jump to Chapter 6 for an in-depth dive into how to gain financial independence by 'Becoming your Own Bank')*

---

[2] American Psychological Association, "APA Survey Shows Money Stress Weighing on Americans' Health Nationwide," *American Psychological Association*, February 4, 2015, https://www.apa.org/news/press/releases/2015/02/money-stress.
[3] Consumer Financial Protection Bureau, "Financial Well-Being: The Goal of Financial Education," January 2015, https://files.consumerfinance.gov/f/201501_cfpb_report_financial-well-being.pdf.

Money Says, 'Save Me, I Will Save You!'

As you may have realized by now, savings play a critical role in financial health. I know families who have transformed their lives by managing money effectively.

Having read this far, the impact of financial health on overall well-being becomes somewhat self-evident. The statistics are straightforward: manage money well, and the positive impacts are significant. I firmly believe that money is like a big brother—it should always be there to support you. If you save it, it will save you in the future.

A study[4] by the **Pew Charitable Trusts** found that families with savings of $2,000 (approximately INR 1.7L) are less likely to experience financial hardship compared to those without savings. This underscores the importance of having a financial cushion to fall back on during tough times.

Saving and Spending Wisely

It's not about depriving yourself of your needs or wants but about finding a balance. Saving even 10-20% of your regular income can make a significant difference. Many people chase after money but fail to manage it wisely once they have it. For instance, marketing strategies often entice people to spend on luxury items like cars or handbags when they could be investing in assets that generate income.

The modern world offers numerous conveniences for spending money quickly and effortlessly, from credit cards to digital payment platforms. While these tools can be beneficial as they facilitate spending, they also make it easy to lose track of your expenses. Plastic cards and digital payment methods put your money at your fingertips, but they also encourage impulse buying.

---

[4] The Pew Charitable Trusts, "Are American Families Becoming More Financially Resilient?" *The Pew Charitable Trusts*, April 2017, https://www.pewtrusts.org/en/research-and-analysis/issue-briefs/2017/04/are-american-families-becoming-more-financially-resilient.

I personally avoid using such tools to ensure I remain in control of my finances. Friends often call me mad for not using any digital payment platforms or credit cards, but I prefer to track my spending meticulously. This approach helps me avoid unnecessary expenses and maintain financial discipline.

Banks and marketers often lure customers with the promise of convenience and rewards. However, free credit cards, promotional offers, and easy access to funds can lead to overspending and financial mismanagement. Therefore, it's important to recognize these tactics and stay focused on your financial goals.

The impact of financial stress isn't just limited to personal finances—it can also affect professional life. To illustrate these points further, consider the story of a family who overcame financial struggles through better money management. They were constantly worried about money, even though they earned a good salary. This anxiety affected both their performance at work and their personal life. They were burdened with significant debt and lived paycheck to paycheck. After seeking my advice, we reviewed their "Expenses Chart," and I helped them prioritize their spending. We worked together to implement a financial plan, developing a budget focused on saving and devising a strategy to gradually pay down their debt. This gave them a sense of control over their finances, which significantly reduced their stress and, in turn, improved both their personal and professional lives. Over time, they built an emergency fund and eventually invested in income-generating assets. This transformation not only improved their financial stability but also reduced their stress and enhanced their overall quality of life.

So, what do we learn from this? Effective financial management requires a comprehensive approach that includes budgeting, saving, investing, and avoiding unnecessary debt. It's also important to educate yourself about financial matters and seek professional advice when needed. By taking these steps, you can achieve financial stability and improve your overall well-being.

Paisa Sambhalna is like Lambi Race ka Ghoda

Managing finances effectively is not just about handling current expenses; it's about ensuring long-term financial stability and growth. One of my core principles is to keep minimal liquid cash in my bank account, investing the majority in fixed deposits (FDs) and stocks. This strategy ensures that my money is constantly working for me, earning returns and not just sitting idle.

I've made it a point to pass down the financial wisdom I've learned (from and) to my son, who is now 18. Times have certainly changed from when I was his age. Back then, saving meant keeping cash in a jar or a savings account, but now it's all about stocks and investing. My son has really taken to learning about the stock market. Recently, I gave him a sum of money to invest, and within just 15 days, he managed to make a profit of 25-40% on his initial investment. Watching him take charge of his financial decisions has been a rewarding experience. It reminds me of how my father taught me, though the tools have evolved over time. By teaching him these principles early on, I'm ensuring he understands the importance of financial responsibility and the potential rewards of wise investments. The shift from cash to stocks reflects how financial management has evolved across generations, but the core lessons remain the same.

Over the years, I've noticed that inheriting wealth doesn't always mean people are equipped to manage it. I've encountered individuals from affluent families who had access to significant financial resources but lacked the knowledge or skills to sustain that wealth. Many of these individuals never engaged with their family businesses or took the time to learn long-term money management. As a result, some have faced challenges because they didn't build the financial literacy needed to preserve and grow their wealth. It's a reminder that financial knowledge is just as crucial as having money in the first place.

A notable example is a family I knew well. Despite their extensive education, including MBAs from prestigious universities in the UK and US, they couldn't maintain their inherited businesses. They were unprepared to "bend their back" and put in the necessary hard work. Despite their high educational qualifications, this lack of practical experience and financial management skills led to their downfall.

The lessons my father taught me were rooted in practicality and hard work. When I was young, I used to sweep the floor of our shop every morning. My father insisted that I do this even if the worker would arrive later to clean. He taught me that there is no shame in hard work, especially when it's for your own business. This hands-on approach ingrained in me the value of every aspect of running a business from the ground up.

Many wealthy families fall into the trap of relying solely on their generational wealth, or *'khandani'* pride, without instilling the values of hard work and financial management in their successors. This often leads to the erosion of wealth over time. I've seen families who once had substantial fortunes fall into financial despair because their successors were ill-prepared to manage the wealth.

For instance, our family friends, let's call them the ABCs, were millionaires with a thriving business. The father, Mr. ABC, often compared his sons to me, urging them to learn from my example of working at our family shop. However, his sons were more interested in luxurious lifestyles and leisure activities like gambling their money. After Mr. ABC passed away, his sons were unable to manage the business effectively. They had not acquired the necessary skills or discipline, leading to the decline of their once-prosperous enterprise.

As I have seen it all happen, I want to empower you with years of my knowledge.

Why It is Important to Financially Educate Your Children Early On in Life

Had the brothers been taught financial management early on, their story might have been different. Financial education would have equipped them with the skills to maintain and grow their wealth, even in their father's absence. My own father often recounted stories of the ABCs and their lavish lifestyle, noting how their lack of financial discipline led to their downfall. In contrast, despite similar beginnings, my father's other friend instilled the value of hard work and financial prudence in his children, which made all the difference.

My father was a diligent man who believed in the value of money and the importance of financial management. He taught me practical lessons, emphasizing that no job was beneath us, which kept me grounded throughout life. This instilled a sense of responsibility and work ethic in me from a young age. Unlike the ABC brothers, who were pampered and shielded from financial realities, my father's approach was hands-on and practical, teaching me the hard way how to manage and value money.

I've carried these lessons forward with my own son. When he was seven years old, I gave him 100 rupees and sent him to the store to buy something for himself. To my surprise, he returned with only what he needed, avoiding unnecessary splurges on chocolates or other items. This showed me that he understood the value of money from a young age. This made me realize that 'charity begins at home' and that instilling these values and practices from a young age is what shapes our children into financially responsible adults.

Now, at 18, my son's keen interest in stocks has motivated him to save money. By instilling these principles early on, I'm ensuring that he understands the importance of financial prudence and the benefits of wise investments.

Balancing Frugality (Needs) and Leisure (Wants)

While I now indulge in a few luxuries, such as buying a pair of Louis Vuitton shades or fine Oudh, I still adhere to the principles of financial management my father taught me. My son, despite being a "super rich father's son," values simplicity and practicality. He chooses to have minimal clothing, and when I offer to buy him more, he declines, insisting on making the *most* of what he has before acquiring more. His approach to spending and saving has even taught me a few lessons. For example, he questions why we need more clothes than necessary, pointing out that one only needs enough for a week, plus a few extras for special occasions. I admire and encourage this pragmatic approach to consumption.

The Importance of Financial Discipline and Planning

In our journey of financial management, it's crucial to highlight how personal discipline and meticulous planning play a significant role in ensuring financial stability and happiness. By God's grace, I have reached a point where I can afford some luxuries, but I never lose sight of the financial discipline that brought me here. This lesson applies not only to individuals but also to families.

It's all in the family!

My wife and I come from strong business backgrounds; she is Sindhi, and I am Gujarati. This combination has created a robust financial synergy in our household. Interestingly, despite my initial teachings, I often find myself being the one who spends the most (albeit to save more) while my wife and son remain frugal. Where I handle the business and bring in the income, my wife, despite being from an affluent family, still tends to bargain and ensure we don't spend unnecessarily, keeping our entire family grounded.

This balance has worked well for us, ensuring we save and invest wisely while also enjoying our lives. My life is filled with instances where financial prudence has led to significant benefits. Many people in our community share my approach to money management. These real-life examples highlight the connection between good money management and personal happiness.

The link between good money management and personal happiness is straightforward yet profound. When you manage your finances well, you can meet your basic needs, provide for a good education, and even enjoy luxuries like vacations without stress. This approach allows you to fulfill your desires without compromising your financial stability.

Planning for Happiness

To illustrate, let's consider planning for a vacation. Suppose you decide to travel in December and start saving specifically for that trip from January. By the time December arrives, you will have a dedicated travel fund, ensuring that your trip does not disrupt other financial commitments. This method brings immense personal happiness as you enjoy your vacation without financial worries. *(Jump to Chapter 5 for an in-depth dive into the concept of 'Boxes').*

A Practical Example: Our Trip to the USA

In 2016, my family and I planned a trip to the USA. The entire budget for our 29-30 day trip was substantial, but we began saving for this vacation in 2015, ensuring that we had the necessary funds without straining our finances. We meticulously planned every detail, from hotels to shopping budgets. Upon arrival in Chicago, where our relatives live, we stuck to our budget. I clearly outlined the spending limits for shopping and other activities for my wife, my son, and myself. This disciplined approach ensured that we enjoyed our vacation to the fullest without any financial stress or the burden of paying it back later with heavy interest.

In our household, we maintain clear financial boundaries. My wife and I have a mutual understanding and respect for each other's finances. If either of us needs money, we provide it without hesitation, but we also adhere to our financial limits. This clarity and mutual respect have been fundamental to our financial harmony and success.

Our trip to Chicago highlighted the importance of financial planning and discipline. On the second day, my relative remarked that I must be stressed about paying bills when I returned home. I found this amusing and clarified that we had meticulously planned and saved for this trip since 2015. My wife laughed and confirmed that I managed everything with savings and only used a credit card for internal travel expenses, such as taxis, where cash wasn't accepted. This meant I enjoyed our vacation hassle-free without worrying about anything upon our return.

My relative's comments shed light on a prevalent issue in both the US and India: many people spend money they don't have, relying on credit to finance their lifestyles. This mentality, exacerbated by the pandemic, has led to a dangerous trend where immediate gratification overshadows financial prudence. People often believe that since life is short, they should spend freely, but this mindset can lead to financial instability and a lack of respect from others.

The issue with this thinking is that it often leads people to use credit to fund their lifestyle. During the pandemic, this tendency worsened as people tried to 'live in the moment,' possibly out of stress or fear of the future. But constantly focusing on instant gratification instead of being responsible with money can cause real problems down the road.

In my view, the "spend now, worry later" attitude can be dangerous. While it may feel good at the moment, it often leads to financial instability later. Without savings, investments, or a plan for the future, it's easy to end up in debt and struggle to make ends meet. Plus, this mindset can cause people to lose respect for you. When they see that you're constantly relying on credit or living beyond your means, it can make them question your ability to handle not just money but life in general.

Being responsible with money doesn't mean you can't enjoy life—it just means finding a balance. You can have fun and live in the moment, but it's important to plan for your future, too. The goal is to enjoy life today without risking your security tomorrow.

The Harsh Reality of Financial Respect: 'Paisa Hai Toh Izzat Hai'

How does money affect your affluence?

Money undeniably influences social interactions. As the saying goes, "Money talks." And indeed, when money talks, vocabulary doesn't seem to matter. People respect and pay attention to those who are financially successful, regardless of their other qualities. The King of Bollywood, who rose from a middle-class background to stardom in Mumbai, underscores the crucial role of money in life. He remarks, "Money is not everything in life. But it makes life one hell of an easier place to be in if you have a lot of it." His perspective resonates with many, as financial stability often dictates how one is perceived and treated by others.

One of my habits is always inquiring about my friends' financial well-being. A common question I ask is, "Is money coming in or going out this month?" While this might sound materialistic, it's a pragmatic approach in today's world, where financial security is paramount.

When I discuss finances, I often encounter a range of opinions on the role money plays in life. Some people downplay its importance, brushing it off by saying, "Money comes and goes," almost as if it's not worth stressing over. While I understand that life can be unpredictable and that there's more to it than just money, I personally believe that both saving and spending wisely are crucial. It's not just about how much you earn but how you manage it—balancing between enjoying the present and planning for the future.

In my circle, conversations about money come up quite often, and I find it interesting to see how people view financial success. When someone in the group says, "Yes, the money is coming in" (meaning things are going well), it gives me a sense of satisfaction and contentment. It's not just about the money itself but knowing that those around me are making smart financial decisions and are on track to do well. It's a sign that people are not only earning but also managing their finances in a way that sets them up for stability and growth. That's a conversation I'm always happy to have— because it shows that, in my circle, people understand the value of being financially responsible.

Ultimately, financial security offers stability and peace of mind. People who spend recklessly often do so to impress others, but this behavior leaves them vulnerable and unsupported in times of need. The only reliable support in such situations is one's own savings. Therefore, it is crucial to manage money wisely, saving where possible and spending thoughtfully to ensure long-term security and respect.

In times of crisis, you may find that nobody is there to support you. Even those who once enjoyed your generosity may not come to your aid. If you ask anyone—be it a friend, family member, or even your parents—for a small sum like 1000 rupees, you're likely to face a barrage of questions. Your father might question your needs, and your mother will likely do the same.

In today's world, where relationships are increasingly built on the foundation of money, losing that financial stability often means losing those connections. This reality underscores the importance of financial independence and prudent money management.

Personal Experiences with Financial Stress

I've seen both professionals and businessmen face burnout due to financial stress. A notable example is from my own experience. At 16, I was taught to live within my means despite having super-rich friends and family. However, at 17, I faced a setback when I flunked an economics exam. Disappointed, my father sent me to Gujarat to work in Alang, a ship-breaking yard near Bhavnagar, under the supervision of my mother's cousin.

Alang is renowned for its ship-breaking industry, where massive financial transactions occur over short periods. Businessmen there often take out substantial loans, break down ships, and turn over significant profits within months. During my eight to nine months in Alang, I witnessed firsthand the importance of financial discipline and the immense potential for wealth creation through strategic planning and hard work.

This experience was transformative, teaching me valuable lessons about financial management that ultimately shaped my approach to money. By planning meticulously and living within my means, I learned to manage my finances effectively, avoiding the pitfalls of debt and financial stress. This approach not only helped me avoid burnout but also allowed me to enjoy financial stability and personal happiness.

The connection between good money management and personal happiness is undeniable. Proper financial planning ensures that you can meet your needs and achieve your desires without undue stress. For example, saving gradually for a planned vacation ensures that you can enjoy your trip without worrying about the financial implications.

It's essential to maintain financial discipline, even when indulging in occasional luxuries. Understanding the difference between wants and needs, setting aside savings for specific goals, and avoiding unnecessary debt are key strategies for financial well-being.

Financial management is crucial for personal happiness and stability. Learning from experiences, whether your own or those of others, can provide valuable lessons in managing money effectively. By planning ahead, living within your means, and saving for future needs, you can achieve financial independence and enjoy a secure and fulfilling life.

In This Chapter...

We've explored the impact of money on health, relationships, and opportunities, highlighted common financial challenges, and discussed the benefits of good money management. It's crucial to understand that managing your finances wisely is not just about accumulating wealth—it's about creating a balanced and fulfilling life. By being your own bank, saving diligently, and spending wisely, you can ensure financial stability and peace of mind, ultimately leading to a happier and more fulfilling life.

The essence of financial management lies in discipline, planning, and mutual respect. By teaching these values to our children and practicing them in our daily lives, we ensure economic stability and happiness. Whether it's saving for a vacation or managing daily expenses, a well-planned financial strategy brings peace of mind and personal fulfillment. This approach, rooted in practical experience and family values, creates a strong foundation for future generations.

Financial discipline and planning are not just about saving money but also about securing a stable and respectful life. By planning ahead, managing expenses, and understanding the true value of money, one can enjoy life without financial stress. These principles have guided my family and me, allowing us to live comfortably and responsibly.

Reflect on your current financial situation and identify any challenges or stress points. Commit to learning and applying the money management strategies discussed in this book to improve your financial well-being.

By acknowledging the crucial role of money management, you've taken the first step toward financial confidence and a balanced life. In the next chapter, we'll dive into setting clear and achievable financial goals, ensuring that your dreams and desires are within reach.

"PAISA SAMBHALNA IS LIKE LAMBI RACE KA GHODA"

-Anand Mehta

₹2
MASTERING FINANCIAL GOALS

FAQ

Q: When should one spend, and how should they approach it?

Spend when it doesn't leave a lingering worry in the back of your mind or when you won't regret the purchase tomorrow. Financially healthy spending is something you can repeat with peace of mind. Spending should bring you joy, not anxiety; if you need to think twice about affording something, perhaps it's worth saving for a bit longer.

"Planning is bringing the future into the present so that you can do something about it now."

— Dr. Raghuram Rajan, Economist

Imagine you're on a road trip with no destination. Your car hums along the highway, but instead of feeling excited, you grow increasingly frustrated. You drive aimlessly, taking random turns, unsure of your destination or when you'll arrive. Watching the fuel gauge drop steadily, you know you're wasting time and resources. Eventually, you pull over, exhausted and no closer to anything meaningful.

This scenario is akin to managing your finances without clear goals. It's easy to find yourself stuck in a cycle of earning and spending with no real sense of progress or purpose. Just as a road trip requires a destination to be fulfilling, your financial journey needs well-defined goals to give it direction and meaning.

You need a roadmap to reach your dream financial destination—whether it's buying a home, retiring comfortably, or achieving financial independence. This roadmap isn't just a rough sketch; it's a detailed plan that guides your decisions and actions, ensuring every step moves you closer to your goals. With a clear destination, you can prioritize your spending, save strategically, and invest wisely.

Imagine the relief of knowing that every mile you drive and every dollar you earn is bringing you closer to a life of financial security and freedom. With the right goals in place, you can confidently navigate life's twists and turns, making informed choices that lead you to your desired financial future.

Setting financial goals is crucial for effective money management. Without clear goals, it's easy to lose track of where your money is going, leaving you unprepared for both expected and unexpected expenses. Financial goals provide direction and purpose, helping you make decisions that align with your values and aspirations.

This chapter will guide you through identifying, prioritizing, and setting realistic financial goals. Whether your aim is to save for a significant purchase, pay off debt, build an emergency fund, or plan for retirement, having clear objectives will empower you to take control of your finances.

We'll explore how to balance your short-term desires—like buying that new gadget or taking a vacation—with your long-term needs, such as securing your financial future or providing for your family. By the end of this chapter, you'll have the tools and strategies to create a personalized financial roadmap that helps you achieve your goals and live the life you envision.

Establishing these goals is not just about numbers on a page; it's about creating a sustainable financial plan that reflects your priorities and sets you up for success. Whether you're just starting your financial journey or looking to refine your plans, this chapter will provide the guidance you need to ensure a secure and prosperous future.

Types of Financial Goals:

Financial goals are the building blocks of a solid financial plan. Like a well-crafted building needs a strong foundation, your financial future requires clearly defined goals. These goals can be categorized into three main types: short-term, medium-term, and long-term. Understanding the differences between these categories and how they fit into your overall financial strategy is the first step toward achieving financial success.

Short-term goals are those you aim to accomplish within a year or two. These include saving for a vacation, building an emergency fund, paying off small debts, or purchasing a new appliance. Short-term goals are often more immediate and easier to achieve, but they are just as important as long-term ones. They provide quick wins that can motivate you to stay on track and demonstrate the power of financial discipline.

Medium-term goals generally have a time horizon of two to five years. These goals require more planning and saving but are still within reach in the not-too-distant future. Examples of medium-term goals might include saving for a down payment on a house, funding a child's education, or paying off significant debts like a car loan. Achieving these goals often requires balancing your current lifestyle with your future aspirations, making careful budgeting and consistent savings essential.

Long-term goals are the major milestones you aim to achieve in more than five years. These include planning for retirement, paying off your mortgage, or building a substantial investment portfolio. Long-term goals require patience, perseverance, and a long-term commitment to your financial plan. They often involve larger sums of money and a greater degree of planning, but the payoff can be life-changing.

Identifying these goals is the first step toward financial success. Start by inventorying what you want to achieve in each timeframe. Consider your current financial situation, your future aspirations, and the lifestyle you want to maintain. Write down your goals, and be as specific as possible. For example, instead of setting a vague goal like "save money," aim for something concrete like "save ₹10,000 for a down payment on a house within three years."

Once you've identified your goals, you can begin to prioritize them. Depending on your circumstances, some goals might be more urgent or important than others. For instance, building an emergency fund might take precedence over saving for a vacation if you don't have a financial safety net. Prioritizing your goals will help you focus your resources where they're needed most and ensure that you're progressing toward the things that matter most to you.

By clearly identifying your financial goals and understanding their timeframes, you lay the groundwork for a financial strategy that aligns with your values and aspirations. This process gives you a clear sense of direction and empowers you to take control of your financial future with confidence and clarity.

Financial goals can generally be divided into three categories: short-term, medium-term, and long-term. Each type serves a different purpose in your financial planning and requires a different approach.

Let's understand this better with the following case study.

Case Study: Understanding Financial Goals through Mira's Journey

Mira is a 30-year-old graphic designer living in a bustling city. She earns a steady income, but like many, she's been living paycheck to paycheck. Mira has decided it's time to take control of her finances and set concrete financial goals.

- **Short-Term Goals:** Mira's priority is to build an emergency fund. She realizes she needs at least three months' worth of living expenses saved up to protect herself against unexpected financial shocks, such as a job loss or medical emergency. She sets a goal to save ₹600,000 over the next year by putting aside ₹50,000 per month.

She also wants to pay off her credit card debt, which stands at ₹300,000. To do this, she creates a plan to allocate ₹30,000 per month toward paying off this debt, aiming to be debt-free within ten months.

- **Medium-Term Goals:** Mira has always dreamed of owning her own home. She knows she'll need a substantial down payment to make this dream a reality. She sets a medium-term goal to save ₹3,000,000 over the next four years for a down payment. To reach this goal, Mira plans to save ₹62,500 per month in addition to her short-term savings efforts.

Another medium-term goal is to upgrade her car. Her current vehicle is reliable but is starting to show its age. Mira estimates she'll need ₹1,000,000 for a decent upgrade. She plans to save ₹20,000 per month over the next four years to reach this goal.

- **Long-Term Goals:** Looking further ahead, Mira knows she needs to start planning for retirement. She sets a long-term goal of building a retirement fund that will provide her with ₹1 crore by age 65. She contributes ₹50,000 per month to her retirement account to reach this goal.

Mira also longs to start her own graphic design business. Knowing this will require a significant investment, she sets a goal to save ₹10,000,000 over the next 10 years to cover startup costs and initial operations.

By setting these goals, Mira has created a clear roadmap for her financial journey. Each goal—short-term, medium-term, or long-term—serves a specific purpose and helps her stay focused on what's most important. With her goals in place, Mira is better equipped to make informed financial decisions, track her progress, and ultimately achieve the financial success she's been striving for.

The Importance of Identifying Financial Goals

Identifying what matters most to you financially is crucial for several reasons. Understanding your financial priorities allows you to make informed decisions, stay focused on your long-term goals, and achieve financial security and satisfaction. Here's why it's so important:

1. Alignment with Personal Values
- **Consistency in Decision-Making:** When your financial goals align with your core values, your financial decisions reflect what truly matters to you. This alignment helps you avoid decisions that might bring short-term satisfaction but conflict with your long-term objectives.
- **Sense of Purpose:** Knowing what matters most gives your financial journey a sense of purpose and direction. It transforms your financial goals from mere numbers into meaningful milestones that reflect your aspirations and beliefs.

2. Focused Financial Planning

- **Prioritization of Resources:** Identifying your financial priorities effectively helps you allocate your resources—time, money, and energy. You're more likely to focus on truly important goals rather than spreading yourself thin across less meaningful objectives.
- **Avoiding Financial Overwhelm:** With clear priorities, you can avoid the stress of trying to achieve too many financial goals at once. This focus allows you to progress steadily on what matters most rather than feeling overwhelmed by competing demands.

3. Motivation and Commitment

- **Sustained Motivation:** When your financial goals are closely tied to what you value most, you're more likely to stay motivated and committed to achieving them. This connection helps you persevere through challenges, as you know the result is deeply meaningful to you.
- **Achieving Satisfaction:** When completed, goals that resonate with your values bring greater fulfillment. This satisfaction can reinforce positive financial behaviors and encourage you to strive toward other important goals.

4. Balanced Financial Life

- **Short-Term vs. Long-Term Balance:** Understanding what matters most helps you balance short-term desires with long-term needs. For example, you may delay a luxury purchase in favor of saving for retirement because financial security in the future is more important to you.
- **Avoiding Regret:** By focusing on what's truly important, you reduce the risk of future regret. Decisions made without a clear understanding of your priorities can lead to outcomes that may not satisfy you in the long run.

5. Financial Security and Peace of Mind

- **Building a Secure Future:** Prioritizing goals like saving for retirement, paying off debt, or creating an emergency fund ensures you're prepared for the future. This focus on essential goals provides financial security and peace of mind, knowing you're on a path that supports your well-being.

- **Managing Financial Risks:** Knowing what's most important, you're better equipped to protect those priorities from potential financial risks. For instance, you might prioritize health insurance or an emergency fund because your family's health and security matter most.

6. Effective Use of Limited Resources
- **Maximizing Return on Investment:** Financial resources are often limited, so using them wisely is crucial. By identifying what matters most, you can direct your investments and savings toward goals that will bring the greatest return on investment in terms of personal satisfaction and future stability.
- **Avoiding Wasted Efforts:** Without clear priorities, you might spend time and money on things that don't align with your long-term goals. Identifying what matters most helps you avoid unnecessary expenditures and focus on what will benefit you the most.

7. Adaptability to Life Changes
- **Flexible Goal Setting:** Life circumstances and priorities can change over time. Regularly reassessing what matters most to you financially allows you to adapt your goals to reflect new realities, ensuring that your financial plan remains relevant and effective.
- **Navigating Transitions:** During major life changes—such as marriage, having children, or changing careers—knowing your financial priorities helps you navigate these transitions smoothly, ensuring that your financial decisions continue to support your overall life goals.

8. Enhanced Financial Relationships
- **Alignment with Partners or Family:** If you share financial responsibilities with a partner or family, identifying mutual financial priorities can help prevent conflicts and ensure everyone is working toward common goals.
- **Clear Communication:** When you're clear about what matters most, you can effectively communicate your financial goals and priorities, leading to better collaboration and

understanding among those involved in your financial decisions.

The foundation for effective financial planning is identifying what matters most to you financially. It ensures that your financial decisions are purposeful, aligned with your values, and focused on achieving long-term satisfaction and security. This clarity enhances your financial well-being and brings peace of mind, knowing that you're working toward a future that truly reflects your aspirations.

Identifying Financial Goals: A Guide

1. Assess Your Current Financial Situation
- **Review Your Finances:** Start by taking a comprehensive look at your current financial situation. This includes understanding your income, expenses, debts, savings, and investments.
- **Identify Your Strengths and Weaknesses:** Recognize areas where you're doing well (e.g., consistent savings, low debt) and areas where you need improvement (e.g., high credit card debt, lack of an emergency fund).

2. Reflect on Your Values and Priorities
- **Consider What Matters Most to You:** Your financial goals should align with your values and life priorities. Reflect on what's important to you: financial security, family, travel, education, or retirement.
- **Think Long-Term and Short-Term:** While focusing on immediate needs is easy, consider your long-term aspirations. Balancing short-term desires with long-term needs is essential for a well-rounded financial plan.

3. Envision Your Ideal Future
- **Visualize Where You Want to Be:** Imagine your life five, ten, or even twenty years from now. Where do you see yourself living? What kind of lifestyle do you want? What major milestones do you want to achieve?
- **Consider Major Life Events:** Think about significant life events that may require financial planning, such as buying a home, starting a family, pursuing further education, or retiring.

4. Categorize Your Goals

- **Short-Term Goals:** These are goals you aim to achieve within the next year or two, like building an emergency fund, paying off small debts, or saving for a vacation.
- **Medium-Term Goals:** These goals have a timeframe of two to five years and might include saving for a down payment on a house, funding education, or paying off larger loans.
- **Long-Term Goals:** These are goals that extend beyond five years, such as retirement planning, paying a mortgage, or starting a business.

5. Make Your Goals Specific

- **Be Clear and Concrete:** Instead of setting vague goals like "save money," make your goals specific, measurable, and time-bound. For example, "save $10,000 for a down payment on a house within three years."
- **Set Realistic Expectations:** Ensure your goals are achievable based on your current financial situation and projected income.

6. Prioritize Your Goals

- **Rank Your Goals:** Some goals will be more urgent or important than others. Prioritize them based on your immediate needs and long-term aspirations.
- **Balance Competing Goals:** If you have multiple goals, you may need to balance them by allocating resources appropriately, such as splitting your savings between an emergency fund and a retirement account.

7. Evaluate and Adjust Regularly

- **Review Your Goals Periodically:** Life circumstances can change, so it's essential to review and adjust your financial goals. Revisit your goals annually or whenever a significant life event occurs.
- **Stay Flexible:** Be willing to adjust your goals as needed. If your financial situation improves or worsens, you may need to revise your goals accordingly.

Case Study: Priya's Financial Planning Journey

Financial Planning Case Study: Priya's Strategy

Priya is a 28-year-old software engineer living in Bangalore. With five years of work experience, she is now focused on optimizing her income and preparing wisely for the future.

1. Assessing Current Financial Situation: Priya earns ₹12 lakhs per annum and has saved ₹3 lakhs in a savings account. Her recurring expenses include a car loan of ₹5 lakhs and monthly rent of ₹25,000. Additionally, she has ₹50,000 in credit card debt.

2. Reflecting on Values and Priorities: Priya values financial independence and is committed to supporting her aging parents. She loves traveling and is keen on building wealth through investments. With potential marriage plans in the next few years, she aims to ensure financial readiness.

3. Envisioning the Future Over the next 5 to 10 years, Priya sees herself purchasing a flat in Bangalore, providing financial support to her parents, traveling internationally, and starting a family. She recognizes the need to focus on long-term investments and retirement planning.

4. Categorizing Goals
- **Short-Term Goals:**
  - **Pay Off Credit Card Debt:** Priya plans to eliminate her ₹50,000 credit card debt within six months.
  - **Build an Emergency Fund:** She aims to save ₹2 lakhs over the next year to cover six months of living expenses.
  - **Buy Health Insurance:** She intends to buy a health policy for herself and her parents within

three months.

- **Medium-Term Goals:**
  - o **Save for a Down Payment on a Flat:** Priya plans to buy a flat in Bangalore in five years, needing ₹20 lakhs for the down payment, saving ₹4 lakhs annually.
  - o **Plan for Marriage Expenses:** Anticipating marriage in three years, she wants to save ₹5 lakhs for wedding expenses.

- **Long-Term Goals:**
  - o **Build a Retirement Corpus:** Priya aims to accumulate ₹3 crores by retirement at 60, investing ₹20,000 monthly in mutual funds and PPF.
  - o **Support Parents Financially:** She plans to allocate ₹10,000 monthly for her parents' expenses, adjusting as necessary.

5. Making Goals Specific
- **Pay Off Credit Card Debt:** Priya will allocate ₹10,000 monthly to clear her debt in five months.
- **Build an Emergency Fund:** She plans to save ₹16,700 monthly for the next 12 months to reach her ₹2 lakhs goal.
- **Save for Down Payment:** She will save ₹33,300 monthly in high-interest accounts or fixed deposits to gather ₹20 lakhs in five years.
- **Invest for Retirement:** She will diversify her investments across ELSS mutual funds, PPF, and NPS, targeting ₹20,000 per month.

6. Prioritizing Goals Priya prioritizes clearing her credit card debt and building an emergency fund before saving for a flat or wedding expenses. She begins with modest retirement investments, planning to increase contributions as her earnings grow.

7. Evaluating and Adjusting Regularly Priya will review her financial goals bi-annually, adjusting her savings and investment strategies in response to income changes, market shifts, and major life events such as marriage or career transitions.

By methodically identifying and prioritizing her financial goals, Priya ensures a balanced approach to meeting immediate needs, achieving long-term aspirations, and securing a stable financial future for herself and her family.

Prioritizing Financial Goals: A Comprehensive Guide

Identifying what matters most to you financially is key to setting meaningful financial goals. This detailed step-by-step guide will help you clarify your financial priorities:

Step 1: Reflect on Your Values
- **Understand Your Core Beliefs:** Start by reflecting on what you consider most important in life—security, freedom, family, education, and personal growth. Your financial goals should be in harmony with these core values.
- **Ask Yourself Key Questions:**
  - What brings you the most satisfaction?
  - What aspects of life are you unwilling to compromise on?
  - How do you want to be remembered?

Step 2: Envision Your Ideal Life
- **Visualize the Future:** Imagine your life in the next 5, 10, or 20 years. Where do you see yourself living? What kind of career and family life do you envision? What personal interests do you wish to pursue?
- **Consider Milestones:** Think about significant life events like buying a home, starting a family, traveling, or retiring. These considerations can help sharpen your focus on what you truly value.

Step 3: Identify Your Life Goals
- **List Your Aspirations:** Write down your major life goals, whether they're related to financial freedom, starting a business, funding education, or retiring comfortably.
- **Prioritize What's Important:** Order these goals by importance, focusing on those that resonate with your values and future vision.

Step 4: Analyze Your Current Financial Situation
- **Assess Your Financial Health:** Review your income, expenses, savings, investments, and debts to gauge your financial status.
- **Identify Financial Strengths and Weaknesses:** Pinpoint areas of success (like steady income or low debt) and areas needing improvement (like high expenses or inadequate savings).

Step 5: Set Clear, Specific Financial Goals
- **Be Specific and Measurable:** Convert your life goals into precise financial targets. For instance, if seeking financial security, aim to build an emergency fund of ₹5 lakhs within 18 months.

- **Categorize Goals by Time Frame:**
  - **Short-Term (1-2 years):** Focus on immediate needs and smaller objectives.
  - **Medium-Term (3-5 years):** Plan for larger goals requiring extensive preparation.
  - **Long-Term (5+ years):** Set sights on major life achievements and retirement.

Step 6: Balance Short-Term Desires with Long-Term Needs
- **Weigh Immediate Gratification Against Future Security:** Strike a balance between enjoying the present and ensuring future stability.
- **Make Trade-Offs:** Adjust goals as needed to prevent short-term desires from undermining long-term success, such as prioritizing emergency savings over immediate luxuries.

Step 7: Evaluate Your Progress Regularly
- **Monitor and Adjust:** Continually review and adjust your financial goals to reflect changes in life circumstances, income, and priorities.
- **Celebrate Milestones:** Acknowledge achievements to stay motivated and committed to your financial journey.

Step 8: Seek Professional Guidance if Needed
- **Consult a Financial Advisor:** If uncertain, consult a financial expert to receive tailored advice and develop a comprehensive plan.

Step 9: Communicate with Loved Ones
- **Discuss Goals with Family:** Ensure that your financial objectives are clear to family members involved in financial planning to avoid conflicts and align efforts.

Step 10: Stay True to Your Values
- **Revisit Your Values Regularly:** As your life changes, periodically reassess your values to ensure your financial goals remain aligned with what's most important to you.

By following these steps, you will clearly understand what matters most financially and set goals that reflect your true values and aspirations. This strategic approach guarantees that your financial decisions are intentional and aligned with the life you aim to build.

Financial Planning: Building a Secure Future

I firmly believe that financial planning is not just about managing money; it's about building a secure future that reflects my values and aspirations. In this century, with a fluctuating global economy and many individuals living paycheck to paycheck, having a comprehensive financial plan is more crucial than ever. With rising living costs, it becomes increasingly challenging to think beyond immediate needs and consider saving for the future.

1. The Importance of Setting Realistic Financial Goals
- **Clarity and Direction:** I stress the importance of setting clear and realistic financial goals. These goals act as my roadmap, providing clarity and direction for my financial

journey. Whether it's buying a home, funding my child's education, or securing a comfortable retirement, having well-defined goals helps me stay focused and motivated despite financial challenges.

- **Achievable Milestones:** I advocate for setting specific, measurable, and attainable goals, such as saving ₹10 lakhs for a down payment on a house within five years. In today's uncertain financial climate, having practical targets ensures that I can make steady progress toward my long-term objectives without overextending myself.

2. **The Role of Budgeting in Financial Planning**
   - **Foundation of Financial Control:** Budgeting is the cornerstone of any successful financial plan, especially when managing daily expenses has become a struggle. A budget provides a clear picture of my income, expenses, and savings, allowing me to allocate resources effectively and live within my means.
   - **Prioritizing Spending:** With rising costs, budgeting helps me prioritize spending based on what truly matters. By distinguishing between needs and wants, I can avoid unnecessary expenses and focus on building savings for the future, even in a tight financial environment.

3. **Saving for the Future: A Key Component of Financial Security**
   - **The Power of Early and Consistent Savings:** Despite the challenge of setting money aside, I emphasize the importance of saving early and consistently. Starting early allows my money more time to grow through compounding, which is crucial for building a secure financial future.
   - **Building an Emergency Fund:** I advocate for creating an emergency fund as a priority. In today's economic instability, having a safety net of at least 3-6 months' worth of living expenses is essential for peace of mind.
   - **Long-Term Investments:** I encourage investing in assets like mutual funds, stocks, or retirement accounts such as PPF or NPS for long-term goals. Given the current economic challenges, balancing risk and return is important, as well as

ensuring my investments align with my risk tolerance and time horizon.

4. **Aligning Financial Planning with Long-Term Goals**
   - **Goal-Oriented Planning:** Every financial decision should be made with long-term goals in mind. In an economy where immediate needs often overshadow future planning, aligning financial choices with my aspirations is crucial. This ensures that I am consistently working toward a future that reflects my values.
   - **Adapting to Life Changes:** Life circumstances and priorities can change, especially in unpredictable economic times. I regularly revisit and adjust my financial plan to ensure it remains relevant and effective.

5. **The Necessity of a Holistic Financial Plan**
   - **Comprehensive Approach:** I advocate for a holistic financial plan that covers all aspects of financial well-being, including income, expenses, savings, investments, insurance, and estate planning. In a world where many are trapped in short-term thinking, this comprehensive approach ensures that all areas of my financial life work together to support my long-term goals.
   - **Avoiding the Debt Trap:** I also warn against the common trap of using credit to fulfill long-term goals that were not anticipated or planned. This can lead to a cycle of debt that becomes increasingly difficult to escape. By planning and setting realistic goals, I can work toward financial independence and avoid this pitfall.

6. **The Benefits of a Comprehensive Financial Plan**
   - **Peace of Mind:** A solid financial plan provides peace of mind, even in a challenging economic environment. This security allows me to focus on enjoying life, knowing I am prepared for the future.
   - **Achieving Financial Independence:** Ultimately, I see financial planning as the path to financial independence. By setting realistic goals, budgeting effectively, and saving diligently, I can achieve the freedom to live life on my terms without the burden of financial worries.

My perspective on financial planning emphasizes the importance of a thoughtful, goal-oriented approach to managing money. Despite today's economic challenges, setting realistic goals, budgeting wisely, and saving consistently allow me to navigate financial uncertainties and build a secure future that aligns with my long-term aspirations. This comprehensive approach helps achieve financial independence and provides the peace of mind needed to face life's uncertainties.

Understanding Financial Goals

Financial planning and financial goals are intrinsically linked. Financial goals provide the targets and motivation for financial planning, while financial planning offers the framework and strategies needed to achieve these goals. Together, they form a cohesive approach to managing finances, ensuring that resources are utilized effectively to reach desired outcomes and secure a stable financial future.

The Role of Financial Goals: Financial goals are specific objectives that individuals or households aim to achieve within a defined timeframe. They provide direction and purpose to money management efforts, helping to turn abstract dreams into tangible realities. Financial goals can vary widely, ranging from short-term desires to long-term aspirations, and they play a crucial role in shaping financial decisions and strategies.

At their core, financial goals help individuals clarify what they want to achieve financially and establish a roadmap for reaching those objectives. Whether saving for a vacation, purchasing a home, funding a child's education, or planning for retirement, setting clear financial goals transforms broad ambitions into actionable steps. By identifying and prioritizing these goals, individuals can allocate resources effectively, make informed decisions, and stay motivated throughout their financial journey.

The Impact of Financial Goals: Financial goals act as a guiding compass, directing efforts and resources toward meaningful and achievable outcomes. They provide motivation and focus, helping individuals navigate the complexities of money management with confidence and purpose.

Prioritizing Financial Goals: Prioritizing financial goals is a crucial aspect of effective financial planning. Since not all goals can be achieved simultaneously, it's important to determine which goals should take precedence based on urgency, importance, and personal values.

1. **Assessing Urgency:**
   - **Immediate Needs:** Some financial goals require immediate attention due to their urgency. For example, paying off high-interest debt or addressing urgent medical expenses should be prioritized to avoid accruing additional costs or compromising well-being.
   - **Short-Term Requirements:** Goals with approaching deadlines, such as saving for a vacation planned for next year or making a down payment on a car, should be prioritized to ensure they are met on time.

2. **Evaluating Importance:**
   - **Long-Term Security:** Goals that contribute to long-term financial security, such as building an emergency fund, saving for retirement, or investing in education, often hold significant importance. These goals typically have a substantial impact on financial stability and future well-being.
   - **Major Milestones:** Significant life events, such as purchasing a home or funding a child's education, are often deemed highly important. These goals can affect one's quality of life and financial health, making them a priority in financial planning.

3. **Aligning with Personal Values:**
   - **Personal Aspirations:** Goals that align with individual values and life aspirations should be prioritized. For instance, if traveling is a major passion, saving for trips might take precedence over other financial goals.
   - **Family Considerations:** Goals that support family well-being, such as saving for a child's education or planning for

family health expenses, may be prioritized based on their impact on loved ones.

4. **Creating a Hierarchy**
   - **Short-Term vs. Long-Term Goals:** Establish a hierarchy by categorizing goals into short-term, medium-term, and long-term. Short-term goals, such as building a small emergency fund, can be achieved more quickly and should be prioritized to provide immediate financial stability. Medium-term goals, like saving for a down payment, require more time and planning, while long-term goals, such as retirement savings, are crucial for future security but often need more time and sustained effort.
   - **Balancing Immediate and Future Needs:** It's key to strike a balance between addressing immediate needs and working towards future goals. For example, while it's important to manage debt, it's equally important to save for retirement to ensure future financial health.

5. **Evaluating Financial Resources**
   - **Budget Allocation:** Assess how your current budget aligns with your prioritized goals. Allocate funds based on the urgency and importance of each goal. For instance, if debt repayment is a top priority, allocate a larger portion of your budget to pay off debt while making smaller contributions to other goals.
   - **Adjusting Contributions:** Be flexible in adjusting contributions to different goals based on changes in financial circumstances. For example, if a bonus or additional income becomes available, it could be allocated to accelerate progress on high-priority goals.

6. **Setting Milestones and Tracking Progress**
   - **Define Milestones:** Break down large goals into smaller, manageable milestones. For instance, if you're saving for a home, set interim targets, such as saving a certain amount each month. This makes the goal more achievable and allows you to track progress.

- **Regular Reviews:** Periodically review and adjust priorities as needed. Life changes, such as a new job or unexpected expenses, may impact your financial situation and goals. Regular reviews ensure that your priorities align with your current circumstances and objectives.

7. **Seeking Professional Guidance**
    - **Financial Advisor:** Consulting a financial advisor can provide valuable insights if prioritizing goals feels overwhelming or complex. An advisor can help evaluate goals, develop a strategy, and adjust based on evolving financial conditions.

Examples of Prioritizing Financial Goals: Imagine you're juggling several financial goals: building an emergency fund, saving for a family vacation, paying off credit card debt, and contributing to a retirement account. Here's how you might prioritize them.

High-interest credit card debt should be paid off as soon as possible. Paying off this debt will relieve the burden since it is a cost that weighs heavily on finances and is stressful and anxiety-provoking. This becomes your **immediate priority**.

Building an emergency fund is your next step. This fund acts as a safety net for unexpected expenses, eliminating the need for additional credit and providing a sense of security. It's a crucial **short-term goal** on your path to financial independence.

After dealing with debt and establishing an emergency fund, you can start saving for **medium-term goals** like a family vacation. Achieving these goals brings a sense of fulfillment and enhances happiness.

Looking further ahead, your **long-term objective** should be contributing to retirement accounts. This is a key step in planning for your future and can be adjusted based on your other financial priorities.

By carefully evaluating and prioritizing financial goals based on urgency, importance, and personal values, individuals can create a balanced financial plan that addresses immediate needs while working toward long-term aspirations. This helps ensure that resources are allocated effectively and that progress is made toward achieving a secure and fulfilling financial future.

Let's explore a case study that illustrates how understanding and prioritizing financial goals can lead to better resource allocation, ultimately helping individuals achieve a more balanced and fulfilling financial life.

Case Study: Prioritizing Financial Goals in the Context of Annual iPhone Purchases

Ravi, a tech enthusiast, indulges in his passion for the latest technology by purchasing a new iPhone every year, spending approximately ₹1,00,000 annually. While this habit satisfies his desire for the newest gadgets, Ravi has started to question if this expenditure aligns with his broader financial goals and whether these resources could be used more effectively.

Evaluating the Cost and Prioritizing Financial Goals
1. **Assessing the Immediate Financial Goal**
   - **Current Goal:** Owning the latest iPhone annually.
   - **Annual Expenditure:** ₹1,00,000
   - **Total Spent Over 5 Years:** ₹5,00,000

Ravi's immediate financial goal is to keep up with the latest technology. However, he recognizes that this goal might be overshadowing other more impactful financial objectives.

2. **Identifying and Prioritizing Alternative Financial Goals**
   Ravi evaluates how reallocating the ₹1,00,000 spent each year could better serve other financial goals. Here's a comparison in terms of urgency, importance, and personal values:

   - **Investing for the Future**
     - **Goal:** Building long-term wealth through investments.
     - **Annual Investment:** ₹1,00,000
     - **Estimated Growth:** Approximately ₹3,47,000 in mutual funds or stocks over five years.

- o **Priority:** High. Offers significant potential for future financial growth and security.

- **Building an Emergency Fund**
  - o **Goal:** Establishing a financial safety net.
  - o **Annual Savings:** ₹1,00,000
  - o **Total Fund After 5 Years:** ₹5,00,000
  - o **Priority:** High. Provides crucial financial security and peace of mind.

- **Paying Off Debt**
  - o **Goal:** Reducing high-interest debt.
  - o **Annual Repayment:** ₹1,00,000
  - o **Impact:** Saves on interest payments and improves financial health.
  - o **Priority:** High. Critical for financial stability and reducing long-term financial burdens.

- **Education and Skill Development**
  - o **Goal:** Enhancing career prospects and earning potential.
  - o **Annual Investment:** ₹1,00,000
  - o **Priority:** Medium to High. This can lead to significant personal and professional benefits.
- **Travel and Experiences**
  - o **Goal:** Enriching life with meaningful experiences.
  - o **Annual Expenditure:** ₹1,00,000
  - o **Priority:** Medium. Valuable for personal growth but lower priority than financial security goals.

- **Charitable Contributions**
  - o **Goal:** Supporting causes and making a positive impact.
  - o **Annual Donation:** ₹1,00,000
  - o **Priority:** Medium. Aligns with personal values but is considered after more immediate financial needs.

Strategic Financial Decisions By redirecting the ₹1,00,000 spent annually on a new iPhone into higher-priority financial goals, Ravi can achieve more substantial benefits:

- **Investing in the future and building an emergency fund** offers long-term financial growth and security.
- **Paying off debt and investing in education** address pressing financial needs and improve prospects.
- **Traveling and charitable contributions** can be pursued once critical financial goals are met.

By aligning spending with prioritized financial goals, Ravi can make more strategic decisions, ensuring that his resources contribute effectively to both immediate needs and long-term aspirations. This approach enhances overall financial well-being and ensures that personal values and priorities are thoughtfully integrated into financial planning.

In today's world, it's common to find ourselves drawn towards immediate gratifications, such as the latest car, trendy clothes, or dazzling jewelry. These purchases, often driven by emotions and societal pressures, provide a temporary thrill. However, the excitement of new acquisitions typically wanes, turning what was once exhilarating into mere routine.

When we focus exclusively on fulfilling short-term desires, we risk losing sight of more significant, long-term financial objectives. For instance, while the immediate joy of buying a new car or a luxury watch is undeniable, these purchases do little to enhance our future financial stability. In contrast, long-term financial planning embraces a mindset that prioritizes delayed gratification and foresight.

Consider the impact of consistently saving even modest amounts. For example, setting aside just one rupee a day leads to ₹365 in a year and accumulates substantially over a decade. This simple example shows how small, regular savings can significantly impact when viewed through a long-term lens.

The main challenge is shifting focus from the allure of immediate desires to the benefits of long-term planning. Many people find themselves trapped in a cycle of spending on fleeting pleasures without considering the long-term ramifications. This lack of vision for the future often leads to inadequate financial preparation.

To disrupt this cycle, it is crucial to prioritize strategic financial planning. Every expenditure should be scrutinized not only for its immediate satisfaction but also for how it aligns with long-term financial goals. Cultivating a habit of saving and investing, even in small amounts, paves the way to greater financial security and opportunities ahead.

Here are strategies to help maintain this balance:

1. **Evaluate Each Purchase:** Ask whether this purchase is merely for instant gratification or if it contributes to your long-term goals.
2. **Establish Clear Financial Goals:** Having concrete objectives for the future can help steer decisions away from impulsive spending.
3. **Practice Delayed Gratification:** Learn to wait and save for big purchases instead of succumbing to the temptation of credit or impulse buys.
4. **Regular Financial Reviews:** Periodically assessing your financial situation can keep you on track and allow you to make adjustments as necessary to align with your long-term objectives.

While short-term desires can be compelling, they often divert us from achieving more meaningful, long-term goals. By adopting a forward-thinking approach to financial planning, we are better equipped to make informed decisions that ensure our resources contribute to lasting value and stability. Emphasizing long-term financial security over short-lived pleasures enables us to build a foundation for a more stable and prosperous future.

Balancing Short-Term Desires with Long-Term Financial Needs

Life is a delicate balance between seizing the moment and planning for the future. On one hand, short-term desires such as purchasing a new gadget or taking a spontaneous trip bring immediate pleasure and excitement. On the other hand, long-term financial needs, like saving for retirement or buying a home, require careful planning and patience.

Start by Acknowledging Your Short-Term Desires

It's natural to want to enjoy life's little luxuries, but it's important to ensure these desires don't overshadow your long-term goals. Create a budget that allocates a portion of your income to short-term indulgences while reserving a significant portion for your long-term needs. For instance, you might set aside a specific amount each month for a fun activity or purchase while contributing to savings and investments for future goals.

Implement a "Spending Plan"

Categorize your expenses into three categories: needs, wants, and savings.

- **Needs** are essential expenditures like housing and groceries.
- **Wants** include discretionary items such as dining out or entertainment.
- **Savings** encompass contributions to retirement accounts, emergency funds, and major future purchases.

By clearly defining and prioritizing these categories, you create a balanced approach that allows for enjoyment today without compromising your financial health tomorrow.

Practice Mindful Spending

Before making a purchase, ask yourself if it aligns with your long-term goals and if it is worth the trade-off. For example, if you're contemplating a new luxury item, consider whether this expense might delay or impact a significant future goal. This reflection helps you make more deliberate choices, ensuring that your spending supports your immediate happiness and future well-being.

Set Financial Goals that Blend Short-Term Pleasures with Long-Term Security

Plan for vacations and other pleasurable experiences in a way that fits within your overall financial strategy. This allows you to enjoy the moment without jeopardizing your financial future. Integrating immediate and future goals into your financial plan creates a harmonious balance that enriches your present while securing your future.

Ranking Financial Goals

Navigating your financial journey can sometimes feel like steering through a stormy sea of impulses, where every wave of impulse spending threatens to push you off course. Ranking your financial goals acts like charting a steady course with a well-defined map. By prioritizing your goals, you create a structured path that guides your decisions and keeps you focused on what truly matters. This structured approach helps you see beyond the immediate allure of quick purchases and focus on meaningful achievements. It transforms your financial journey from a chaotic scramble into a purposeful expedition, where each step is deliberate and aligned with your long-term aspirations.

By establishing a balance between immediate desires and long-term planning, you can achieve a fulfilling financial life that allows you to enjoy the present while building a stable foundation for the future. Through thoughtful budgeting, mindful spending, and strategic goal-setting, navigating and achieving your most important dreams becomes not just possible but a rewarding part of your everyday life.

Navigating your financial journey requires a structured approach to ensure that both immediate pleasures and long-term aspirations are met. Here's a comprehensive guide on how to effectively rank your financial goals and allocate resources efficiently:

1. **List All Your Financial Goals:** Start by documenting every financial goal you have, regardless of the time frame:
   - **Short-term:** Such as buying a new gadget.
   - **Medium-term:** Like saving for a vacation.
   - **Long-term:** For instance, retirement savings.

2. **Define Each Goal Clearly:** For each goal, clearly specify what you aim to achieve and by when. Examples:
   - "Save ₹2,00,000 for a vacation by December 2025."
   - "Build an emergency fund of ₹5,00,000 within 2 years."

3. **Assess the Urgency:** Evaluate how soon you need to achieve each goal:
   - **High Urgency:** Goals needing achievement within the next year.
   - **Medium Urgency:** Goals planned for the next 2-3 years.
   - **Low Urgency:** Goals that are more than three years away.

4. **Evaluate the Importance:** Reflect on the significance of each goal in terms of your overall financial health and personal satisfaction:
   - **Questions to consider:**
     o How crucial is this goal for my future?
     o Does this goal align with my values and priorities?
   - **Importance Rankings:**
     o **High Importance:** Critical for long-term security or aligning with personal values.
     o **Medium Importance:** Beneficial but not vital.
     o **Low Importance:** Desirable but not essential.

5. **Determine the Financial Impact:** Analyze the financial influence of each goal:
   - **High Impact:** Major goals that significantly affect your financial stability, like buying a home or retirement savings.
   - **Medium Impact:** Goals that enhance financial health but are less critical, such as saving for a car.
   - **Low Impact:** Goals with minimal financial consequences, like occasional luxury purchases.

6. **Rank Goals:** Combine the assessments of urgency, importance, and financial impact to prioritize your goals:
   - **Top Priority:** Goals that are urgent, important, and have a high financial impact.
   - **Medium Priority:** Goals with medium urgency and importance and moderate financial impact.
   - **Lower Priority:** Goals with low urgency, importance, or financial implications.

7. **Create an Action Plan:** Develop a strategy to achieve your top-priority goals first. Allocate resources such as time, money, and effort accordingly. Adjust your budget and savings plans to focus on these prioritized goals.
8. **Review and Adjust Regularly:** Regularly reevaluate your financial goals and their rankings. As life circumstances and priorities shift, it's crucial to adapt your goals and strategies to stay aligned with your evolving needs.

Balancing Immediate and Future Financial Needs

Achieving a balance between enjoying the present and securing the future is essential for a holistic financial strategy. This approach is similar to navigating through two interconnected landscapes: the vibrant present and the tranquil future. Each landscape offers unique rewards and challenges, and harmonizing them is key to a fulfilling and secure financial journey.

By following these steps, you can ensure that your financial decisions are both strategic and adaptable, leading to a well-rounded and prosperous financial life.

Enjoying the Present:

The present offers myriad opportunities for enjoyment and happiness, from indulging in hobbies to dining out or treating yourself. While these experiences are crucial for well-being, they can also lead to quick overspending if not checked by financial restraint. The excitement of the moment can often overshadow the longer-term consequences of spending.

Securing the Future:

Planning for the future involves preparing for significant life events and building a safety net that ensures financial stability. This includes goals like saving for retirement, creating an emergency fund, and investing for future milestones. These actions, while sometimes feeling distant, are essential for maintaining long-term financial health. However, an excessive focus on the future may lead to missed opportunities for present enjoyment.

The Balancing Act:

Achieving a successful financial balance involves several key steps:

1. **Set Clear Priorities:**
   - Define what is important both now and later. Distinguish between immediate goals (like purchasing a new gadget or planning a vacation) and long-term objectives (such as buying a home or planning for retirement).
   - This clarification helps in effectively allocating resources to fulfill both present desires and future needs.

2. **Create a Budget:**
   - Develop a budget that accommodates both your short-term and long-term financial needs.
   - Allocate a portion of your income to enjoy present activities while consistently contributing to savings and investments for future plans.
   - A well-structured budget is pivotal in managing your spending and saving in a balanced manner.

3. **Practice Mindful Spending:**
   - Before making any purchase, consider if it aligns with your long-term goals and assess its value against its cost.
   - This promotes deliberate spending and allows you to enjoy the present without jeopardizing your future financial security.

4. Set Achievable Goals:
- Establish financial targets that allow for short-term enjoyment without compromising long-term security.
- For example, plan for a vacation by setting aside money gradually, ensuring the expense doesn't disrupt your broader financial plans.

5. Review and Adjust Regularly:
- Regularly assess your financial situation and make necessary adjustments to your plan.
- As life circumstances and priorities shift, adapting your financial strategy accordingly is crucial to maintaining balance and seizing new opportunities.

Balancing the enjoyment of the present with securing the future isn't about favoring one over the other; it's about integrating both into a coherent financial strategy. This approach allows you to live a fulfilling life today while laying a stable foundation for tomorrow. By achieving this equilibrium, you ensure that your financial decisions enhance both your immediate happiness and your long-term well-being. This balanced approach not only secures your financial future but also enriches your current life experience.

Setting Realistic and Achievable Financial Goals

Achieving a balance between enjoying the present and securing the future is fundamental to successful financial planning. Establishing realistic and achievable goals is crucial for maintaining motivation and guiding your financial journey toward success.

The Importance of Realistic Goals

Setting goals that reflect your actual circumstances prevents frustration and disappointment that can arise from unrealistic expectations. For example, planning a luxurious vacation without a clear savings strategy or expecting to save a significant amount without adjusting your budget can lead to setbacks.

Strategies for Setting Achievable Goals

1. **Be Specific:** Clearly define your goals. Instead of vaguely aiming to save money, specify the amount and purpose, such as "I want to save ₹50,000 for a vacation by December 2024." This clarity helps in creating a focused plan.
2. **Set a Realistic Timeframe:** Establish a reasonable timeframe based on your current financial situation. If your goal is to save ₹10,000 in the next three months, ensure this is feasible within your budget and spending habits.
3. **Break Down Big Goals:** Divide larger goals into smaller, manageable milestones. For example, if aiming to save ₹1,00,000 for a home down payment, break it into monthly savings of ₹8,333 over a year to make it more attainable and easier to track.
4. **Create a Budget:** Develop a budget that supports your goal. Identify areas for cost-cutting or reallocation to ensure consistent contributions towards your goal. For instance, reducing discretionary spending can help boost your savings rate.
5. **Set SMART Goals:**
   - **Specific:** Clear and detailed.
   - **Measurable:** Quantifiable to track progress.
   - **Achievable:** Realistic, considering your resources and constraints.
   - **Relevant:** Aligns with your broader objectives.
   - **Time-bound:** Includes a specific deadline for completion.
6. **Monitor Progress:** Regularly check your progress. Monthly reviews can help you stay on track and make necessary adjustments.
7. **Celebrate Milestones:** Recognize achievements along the way. Celebrating small successes keeps you motivated and committed to your long-term objectives.
8. **Stay Flexible:** Be prepared to adjust your goals as your financial circumstances change. Flexibility helps you adapt to life's unpredictabilities without straying from your long-term objectives.

Balancing Present Enjoyment and Future Security

Finding the right balance doesn't mean sacrificing immediate pleasures for future stability or vice versa; it involves integrating both aspects into your financial strategy. This approach allows you to enjoy life now while building a stable foundation for the future.

By setting clear, realistic, and measurable goals, you ensure that every step you take is purposeful and achievable. This structured approach not only fosters a sense of accomplishment but also strengthens your overall financial health, paving the way for both present satisfaction and future prosperity.

Case Study: Aarti and Raj

Two people with the same goal - to save money. However, their approaches are different. Let's see a side-by-side comparison of Aarti and Raj's different financial journeys to understand creating financial goals better:

Candidate 1: Raj, a 30-year-old software engineer living in Bangalore. Raj was passionate about his career and enjoyed spending his free time exploring new hobbies and dining out. However, as he approached his thirties, he realized he needed to be more strategic about his finances to ensure long-term stability and fulfillment.

Identifying Goals: Raj began by reflecting on his financial aspirations. He knew he wanted to buy a home, travel more, and build a substantial emergency fund. To make these goals more concrete, he listed them out:

1. **Short-term Goal:** Save ₹1,00,000 for an emergency fund within a year.
2. **Medium-term Goal:** Save ₹5,00,000 for a vacation to Europe in three years.
3. **Long-term Goal:** Save ₹30,00,000 for a down payment on a house in ten years.

Prioritizing Goals: With his goals identified, Raj needed to prioritize them. He recognized that building an emergency fund was critical for financial security and should take precedence. Next, he planned for the vacation, which provided immediate motivation and a tangible reward for his savings efforts. Finally, he focused on the long-term goal of purchasing a home, understanding that this would require sustained effort over many years.

Setting Up a Plan: Raj created a budget that allocated his income towards these goals. He set aside ₹8,000 each month for his emergency fund, ₹4,000 for the vacation fund, and ₹5,000 towards the home down payment. To achieve this, he trimmed discretionary spending by cutting back on dining out and finding more affordable hobbies.

Tracking Progress and Adapting: Each month, Raj reviewed his progress. He used a budgeting app to track his savings and made adjustments when needed. For instance, when he received a job bonus, he redirected part of the money toward his emergency fund to reach his target faster.

Celebrating Milestones: When Raj completed his emergency fund in just ten months, he celebrated with a small weekend getaway. This celebration reinforced his commitment to his financial plan and motivated him to continue working towards his other goals.

Achieving Goals: Three years later, Raj successfully saved ₹5,00,000 for his European vacation, which he enjoyed thoroughly. After ten years of consistent savings, he continued to contribute to his home down payment fund and accumulated enough for a substantial down payment on his dream home.

Candidate 2: Aarti was enthusiastic about her financial future and set ambitious goals for herself. Motivated by success stories she'd read online, she wanted to save ₹20,00,000 within the next two years. Her plan included buying a high-end car and making a substantial down payment on an apartment. She believed she could achieve this by cutting back on all non-essential spending and working extra hours at her job.

The Challenge: Aarti's initial excitement quickly met reality. Her income, although decent, didn't allow for such aggressive savings targets when she factored in her regular living expenses, student loan repayments, and occasional leisure activities. Her plan to save ₹20,00,000 in just two years required setting aside ₹8,33,000 annually, far exceeding what was feasible given her financial situation.

She also realized that her plan to save aggressively for the car and apartment left her with little to no room for emergencies or unexpected expenses. As a result, Aarti felt stressed and overwhelmed. Her budget was stretched thin, and she needed help balancing her financial goals and daily life. The unrealistic nature of her goals led to frustration and burnout.

Adjusting to Attainable Objectives: Recognizing the need for a more practical approach, Aarti decided to reassess her goals. She started by setting more achievable financial objectives. Here's how she adjusted:

1. **Revised Savings Goals**: Aarti recalculated her savings plan based on her income and expenses. She set a new goal of saving ₹5,00,000 over three years. This was a more manageable target, requiring a monthly savings of approximately ₹13,888. This adjustment allowed her to save for a car and apartment over a more extended period.
2. **Emergency Fund First**: Aarti prioritized building an emergency fund. Within the first year, she allocated ₹1,00,000 to this fund, which provided a safety net and reduced her financial stress.
3. **Incremental Goals**: Instead of aiming for a high-end car immediately, Aarti decided to save for a more affordable vehicle. She planned to purchase the car in five years rather than two, allowing her to manage her finances better and avoid compromising her long-term objectives.
4. **Balancing Budget**: Aarti restructured her budget to include a balance of savings, investments, and discretionary spending. This approach helped her enjoy life while steadily working towards her financial goals.

The Outcome: With her revised plan, Aarti felt more in control of her finances. The adjusted goals were within reach, and her stress levels decreased significantly. By focusing on incremental progress and maintaining a balanced budget, she achieved her revised savings target and made meaningful strides toward buying a car and, eventually, an apartment.

Aspect	Aarti	Raj
Initial Goals	Save ₹20,00,000 in two years to buy a high-end car and pay an apartment down.	Save ₹1,00,000 for an emergency fund, ₹5,00,000 for a vacation, and ₹30,00,000 for a home down payment.
Approach	Aggressive and ambitious, focusing on high savings targets and major purchases.	Balanced, with clear short-term, medium-term, and long-term goals.
Challenges Faced	Unrealistic savings target, given her income and expenses. Stress and burnout from stretching her budget too thin.	None; Raj set achievable goals based on his financial situation.
Budgeting	Struggled with a stretched budget and minimal room for emergencies.	Developed a budget that accommodated both short-term desires and long-term needs.

Adjustments Made	Revised her savings goals to ₹5,00,000 over three years. Prioritized building an emergency fund and adjusted her car purchase timeline.	Did not need major adjustments; regularly reviewed progress and maintained flexibility.
Outcome	Successfully adjusted to more attainable goals, reduced stress, and made steady progress toward her objectives.	Achieved his goals as planned, saved for a vacation, built an emergency fund, and purchased a home with his down payment.
Motivation and Success	Initially, she faced frustration but found motivation and success after recalibrating her goals to be more realistic.	Maintained motivation throughout due to clear, realistic goals and incremental achievements.

Summary:
- **Aarti** set overly ambitious goals that initially led to stress and frustration. After reassessing her targets and creating a more manageable plan, she achieved her revised goals and alleviated her financial stress.
- **Raj** approached his financial planning with a balanced strategy from the start. By setting realistic and achievable goals, he managed his finances and steadily progressed toward his short-term and long-term aspirations.

Both individuals learned valuable lessons from their experiences. Aarti's story emphasizes the importance of setting realistic goals and being flexible, while Raj's approach demonstrates the effectiveness of a balanced and well-planned financial strategy.

Financial goal setting is not merely about saving money—it's about crafting a clear and actionable path to ensure financial stability and fulfillment. This chapter delves into the essentials of setting realistic, meaningful financial goals and provides a robust framework for navigating your financial journey effectively.

Establishing a Clear Vision

The process begins with a reflection on what financial success truly means to you. This involves:

1. **Defining Financial Success:**
   - Ask yourself, "What does financial success look like to me?" Is it achieving freedom from debt, accumulating wealth, or perhaps securing a comfortable retirement?
2. **Identifying Long-Term Dreams:**
   - Consider your most significant aspirations: Do you dream of buying a home, traveling extensively, or perhaps retiring early? Clarifying these dreams will help you prioritize your financial goals.
3. **Acknowledging Immediate** Desires:
   - Recognize your short-term wants, such as going on a vacation, purchasing the latest tech gadgets, or paying off your credit card debt. These, too, form part of your financial blueprint.

By reflecting on these points, you articulate a comprehensive picture of your financial desires, both big and small. This reflection serves as the foundation for setting structured and attainable financial goals.

Crafting a Roadmap to Success

Just as a marathon runner plans out each segment of their race, understanding and categorizing your financial goals helps create a strategy that's both feasible and effective.

1. **Categorizing Goals:**
   - Break down your financial targets into short-term, medium-term, and long-term goals. This classification helps in

prioritizing efforts and aligning them with your overall financial timeline.

2. **Setting Clear, Achievable Milestones:**
   - Define each goal with specificity—what do you want to achieve, and by when? For example, instead of merely wanting to "save more money," set a precise target like "save ₹50,000 for an emergency fund within the next year."

3. **Developing a Financial Plan:**
   - Establish a budget that aligns with your goals. Allocate specific amounts towards each goal and adjust your spending habits to support these financial priorities.

4. **Monitoring Progress:**
   - Regularly track your achievements against set milestones. Adjust your strategies as needed to stay on course.

5. **Celebrating Success:**
   - Acknowledge and celebrate each milestone, whether it's reaching a savings target or successfully paying off debt. These celebrations bolster motivation and reaffirm your commitment to your financial journey.

Looking Ahead: Budgeting for Success

With a solid understanding of your financial goals set, the next crucial step is mastering the art of budgeting. Effective budgeting is key to ensuring that you can meet your financial goals without feeling financially constrained. The upcoming chapter will explore advanced budgeting techniques, offering tools and strategies that help manage your finances efficiently, ensuring you remain on track toward achieving your long-term aspirations.

In sum, the journey to financial success is like navigating a well-planned road trip. By setting clear destinations and following a detailed map, you ensure that every financial decision you make is a step towards realizing your dreams. With this structured approach, your financial path is not only clear but also rewarding and enriching.

"LIFE IS FULL OF SURPRISES. SO, STAY CURIOUS"

₹3
THE ART OF BUDGETING

FAQ

Q: Why do you avoid the use of credit or debit cards or make online payments?

For me, there's no real accountability with cards or online spending. Digital transactions make it easy to lose track and spend more than you planned. With cash, I'm mindful and accountable—I see the money physically leave my hand, which creates a tangible sense of control and responsibility.

"You must gain control over your money, or the lack of it will forever control you."

- Dave Ramsey, Financial Advisor

Imagine you're the captain of a ship, navigating through uncharted waters on a quest to discover treasure. The journey ahead is thrilling yet filled with risks. Without a map, you could easily stray off course, run out of essential supplies, or get caught in a sudden storm. Similarly, in personal finance, a budget acts as your essential guide, leading you safely and efficiently toward your financial goals.

Budgeting is not just a tool; it's the cornerstone of successful money management. It involves more than listing your expenses or limiting your spending—it's about fully understanding your financial landscape and making informed decisions to secure your future. Every time you receive income, you face a critical choice: how to distribute these resources in a way that meets your immediate needs while also setting the stage for long-term success. Your budget is the strategy that ensures you're directing your money toward what truly matters, allowing you to live within your means while still planning for your dreams. It's a powerful tool that grants you control over your financial destiny.

This chapter will guide you through creating a budget that aligns with your financial goals and lifestyle. We'll cover various budget types and how to customize them to suit different life stages and priorities. Whether you're starting your financial journey or refining your existing budget, you'll find practical advice and actionable tips to use right away.

We begin by emphasizing the importance of setting clear financial goals. What are you aiming to achieve? Are you saving for a down payment on a house, funding your child's education, or preparing for retirement? By clearly defining your goals, you can develop a budget that addresses your current needs and helps you steadily work toward your long-term objectives.

The Psychology of Money and the Art of Budgeting

Our approach to money extends beyond simple earning and spending; it often reflects our values, relationships, and priorities. Similarly, budgeting is more than a financial exercise—it's a personal statement. It's about using our resources deliberately and aligning our financial decisions with our deepest values. Understanding the psychology behind money enables us to craft a budget that effectively manages our income and expenses while honoring our personal values and long-term goals.

1. **Budgeting as a Reflection of Priorities**
   - The way we allocate money through budgeting mirrors our values. For example, if a significant portion of your income is spent on entertainment and luxury, that indicates where your priorities lie. Conversely, a budget focused on savings, investments, or charitable contributions suggests a mindset geared toward future planning and generosity.
2. **The Emotional Connection in Budget Allocation**
   - Budgeting involves emotional decisions about how to allocate resources. This balance—whether you spend on lifestyle enhancements versus long-term security or save versus share—deeply reflects your beliefs and priorities.
3. **Budgeting: A Tool for Financial Clarity and Control**
   - If money mirrors our character, then a budget frames that reflection, offering clarity and control over our financial future. A well-structured budget should empower you, not restrict you. It's about aligning your finances with your values and using them as a tool for personal growth.

In essence, budgeting allows you to take control of your financial narrative, managing the emotional aspects of spending and saving proactively. It helps alleviate the anxiety of living paycheck to paycheck, providing peace of mind and a sense of purpose.

Understanding the Basics of Budgeting

Budgeting forms the cornerstone of financial stability and long-term planning. It helps individuals and families allocate resources, plan for the future, and ensure that both immediate needs and long-term goals are met. More than just controlling expenses, budgeting fosters financial discipline, informs decision-making, and sets realistic goals for a secure future.

Budgeting transcends simple tracking of income and expenses; it embodies a philosophy of disciplined and thoughtful financial management. A budget allows efficient allocation of resources, ensuring immediate needs are addressed while also planning for the future. Budgeting encompasses everything from managing household expenses to achieving significant life objectives like buying a car or preparing for emergencies.

Importance of a Budget

1. **Financial Control**: A budget provides complete control over your finances by allowing you to monitor where your money goes, ensuring you are not caught off-guard by financial shortages.
2. **Achieving Goals**: It aids in planning for both short-term desires (such as buying the latest gadget or going on vacation) and long-term aspirations (like saving for a home or retirement).
3. **Building Savings**: A well-structured budget integrates savings into your monthly financial routine, enhancing your financial security and preparedness for emergencies.
4. **Avoiding Debt**: By knowing your financial limits, a budget helps prevent overspending and the accumulation of debt, teaching you to live within your means.
5. **Improved Decision-Making**: Understanding the amount of disposable income you have after covering essential expenses can lead to more informed decisions regarding discretionary spending.
6. **Emergency Preparedness**: Effective budgeting includes setting aside funds for unexpected expenses, such as car repairs, medical emergencies, or job loss. This can prevent financial crises from worsening.

7. Peace of Mind: Having a handle on your finances reduces stress and provides peace of mind, knowing that your financial life is well organized.

By providing a financial roadmap, a budget outlines your income, expenditures, savings, and investments over a defined period—typically a month or a year. Think of it as a financial GPS that guides you toward your goals by managing the inflow and outflow of your finances. Without a budget, it's easy to lose track of your spending, especially with various financial commitments like rent, utilities, groceries, and debts. A budget brings structure, ensuring essential expenses are covered, savings goals are pursued, and unnecessary spending is minimized.

Strategic Budgeting for Peace of Mind

I've often observed that people feel stressed about money not because they lack it but because they lack a clear plan for managing it. A budget is your strategy for alleviating financial anxiety. When you precisely understand how much you're saving, spending, and investing, you eliminate uncertainty.

This strategic approach extends beyond mere numbers. Budgeting also involves being mindful of emotional triggers that could prompt poor financial decisions. By setting clear limits and objectives within your budget, you can curb impulsive spending and focus on long-term financial health. It's about proactively shaping your financial circumstances, not merely reacting to them.

Distinguishing Between Needs and Wants:

An essential part of managing expenses is distinguishing between "needs" and "wants." Needs are essential items for survival, such as food, shelter, and healthcare. Wants are non-essential desires, like dining out or purchasing the latest tech gadget. Learning to prioritize needs over wants is crucial for effective budgeting.

A budget is fundamentally a financial plan. But more than that, it's about thoughtful expense management once you receive your money.

Needs vs. Wants: This involves differentiating between essentials, such as groceries or rent, and discretionary spending, like dining out or shopping.

A pivotal moment in my financial journey occurred in 2021. After closing a significant deal, I was tempted to purchase a Mercedes-Benz GLS, a luxury car worth nearly a crore. Despite already owning three cars, social pressures to own a luxury vehicle were mounting. Friends and acquaintances suggested, "With your success, you should be driving a Mercedes." I nearly succumbed, even planning financially by considering placing ₹2.5 crores in a fixed deposit to cover the car's EMI while preserving my savings.

However, I paused to reflect. Did I truly need this car, or was I merely trying to keep up appearances? I opted to modify my existing Ford Endeavour instead, spending ₹10 lakhs to upgrade it, making it as sophisticated as any luxury vehicle. This decision brought immense satisfaction, reinforcing that my self-worth was not tied to a luxury brand. Instead of buying the Mercedes, I invested in property—an investment that has since appreciated significantly.

Reflecting on this decision, I'm thankful I chose long-term value over instant gratification. True financial wisdom lies in making decisions aligned with your long-term goals rather than fleeting desires. This experience taught me that financial prudence isn't about deprivation but about intentional spending. Whether you drive a Maruti, a Hyundai, or a Mercedes doesn't define your success. Wealthy individuals like Mukesh Ambani and Ratan Tata often live modestly relative to their wealth, illustrating that success is not about possessions but about living true to one's values.

When tempted by a significant purchase that may not offer long-term benefits, ask yourself: "Is this a real need, or am I trying to impress others?" Remember, your choices today shape your future, and ultimately, you are solely responsible for your financial well-being.

Components of a Budget: Income, Expenses, Savings, and Investments

A budget is foundational for financial stability and long-term planning. It enables individuals and families to allocate resources, plan for the future, and ensure they can meet immediate needs and long-term goals. A budget is more than just tracking expenses; it's about cultivating financial discipline, making informed choices, and setting realistic goals that secure a stable future.

Budgets vary and can be tailored to fit different aspects of life. For example, a household budget typically includes necessities like groceries, utilities, and transportation—essentials that keep daily life running smoothly. On average, a modest sum each day could suffice for nutritious meals, adequate shelter, and essential utilities. However, budgeting is not one-size-fits-all; it's highly personal and should reflect your unique lifestyle, priorities, and financial situation.

For instance, in a family managed by a couple, one partner might handle daily expenses while the other manages savings and investments. The key is collaboration, ensuring the budget supports both short-term necessities and long-term aspirations. It's about balancing comfort today with security for tomorrow. By understanding your spending patterns and adjusting as needed, you can avoid overspending while still enjoying your income. Budgeting in a family promotes unity and support in achieving financial goals.

Core Components of a Budget:

1. **Income:** This includes all sources of money earned in a given period, not just your salary. Understanding your total income is crucial for setting the limits of your spending, saving, and investing.
2. **Expenses:** These are all the costs incurred over a period, categorized into fixed and variable expenses. Understanding

your expenses is key to maintaining financial control and living within your means.

3. **Savings:** This component of your budget is what you set aside for future needs, whether for emergencies, large purchases, or long-term goals. Establishing a habit of saving ensures you are prepared for both expected and unexpected financial demands.

4. **Investments:** Investments involve putting your money to work to grow over time. Unlike savings, which are typically safer but yield less return, investments carry risk with the potential for higher returns. Balancing your investment portfolio across different asset types can help manage risk and reward.

A well-crafted budget is a dynamic tool that should evolve with changes in your financial situation. Regular reviews and adjustments to your budget are essential for staying on track and avoiding financial issues. Whether you're saving for a home, planning retirement, or simply managing daily expenses, a strategic budget is key to realizing your financial goals.

Adjusting Your Budget Over Time

Life transitions bring new responsibilities and priorities. In my younger years, I received a modest allowance from my father, which afforded me a sense of freedom. When I married in 2002, my allowance was increased to ₹15,000, up from ₹3,000, with the expectation that it would cover all my expenses, including outings with friends and new marital responsibilities.

Before marriage, my social life with well-to-do friends involved lavish spending. Marriage, however, ushered in a new sense of responsibility. I had to scale back on extravagant outings and realign my priorities. My father's financial discipline guided me through these adjustments.

Life changes, and so should your budget. The budget of a single person will differ significantly from that of a married couple with children. It is crucial to revisit and adjust your budget as your life evolves.

Guidelines for Adjusting a Budget:

1. **Review Regularly:** Conduct a budget review at least once a year to reassess your financial flow and adjust for new goals or changes in your financial situation.
2. **Adapt to New Circumstances:** Changes like a growing family, a new job, or economic shifts may require a budget revision to accommodate increased needs.
3. **Prioritize Savings:** As your income increases, so should your savings. Strive to build a financial cushion to avoid relying on loans or credit for emergencies.

My father's approach to budgeting and saving, rooted in prudence despite his wealth, deeply influenced my financial practices. He believed in wisely managing wealth to secure the financial future of subsequent generations.

Creating Your Budget

Budgeting is intensely personal, and various methods can accommodate different lifestyles, financial goals, and income levels. Whether you're saving for a goal, eliminating debt, or tracking expenditures, the key is to choose a budgeting strategy that complements your financial habits.

Steps to Create a Personalized Budget:

1. **Identify Your Income:** Include all sources of earnings, both fixed and variable.
2. **List Your Expenses:** Break down your expenses into essentials (like rent and groceries) and non-essentials (such as dining out and entertainment).
3. **Allocate Funds Strategically:** Use the "box" method to categorize your income, prioritizing essential expenses and allocating the remainder to savings or discretionary spending.

The "box" method is particularly effective; it involves saving in specific categories and only spending when sufficient funds have accumulated, ensuring purchases like a car or vacation are made comfortably without financial strain.

The Box Method

In my financial journey, I've adopted the "box method," which simplifies budgeting by dividing income into designated categories or "boxes." Each box serves a specific purpose, streamlining the management of finances. For example, one box may cover daily necessities like groceries, transportation, and utilities. Another could be set aside for unexpected needs such as medical emergencies or car repairs, while a third might fund lifestyle desires like dining out or traveling.

The key to this method is discipline. Once funds are allocated to a box, they remain there until needed for their specific purpose, preventing you from using money meant for emergencies on non-essential purchases. This disciplined approach aids in effective money management and establishes a financial safety net.

Different Types of Budgets

Budgets can vary based on the different needs and priorities of your life, such as:

1. **Household Budget:**
   - Managed commonly by family members.
   - Covers daily expenses such as groceries, utilities, rent, and transportation.
   - Maintaining a structured household budget ensures that essential expenses are met, reducing financial stress.
2. **Lifestyle Budget:**
   - Includes discretionary spending on entertainment, fashion, and hobbies.
   - The challenge lies in enjoying life without succumbing to financial imprudence.
   - Balances pleasure with discipline to maintain overall financial health.
3. **Emergency Budget:**
   - Acts as a financial buffer for unexpected expenses, preventing disruption to your regular budget or savings.
   - Ideally, cover 3-6 months of living expenses to handle emergencies like medical bills or sudden repairs.

4. Investment & Goal-Oriented Budget:

- Focused on long-term objectives such as buying a home or car or investing in the market.
- Requires careful planning and saving for future financial goals like retirement or children's education.

Using the box method not only categorizes spending and saving but also clarifies financial goals, making it easier to allocate resources effectively and maintain financial stability over time.

Allocating for Generosity: The Role of Discretionary Funds

I've always valued financial generosity, which a well-organized budget can support. Effective money management allows you to help others without compromising your own financial stability. Whether it's lending support to a friend or contributing to charitable causes, having a budget ensures you can afford to give without financial stress.

In my budget, I allocate a portion of my income to discretionary spending. This fund isn't for essentials like bills or savings but for spontaneous acts of generosity or personal treats. Integrating this into your budget allows you to give freely without impacting your financial plans.

Budgeting for generosity offers peace of mind; knowing you have the funds set aside to help others means you can act without financial strain. This approach not only strengthens relationships but also emphasizes that well-managed money should foster connections, not create barriers.

By incorporating both long-term goals and opportunities for generosity into your budget, you transform money from a source of stress into a tool for stability, joy, and community building.

Sticking to a Budget

Adhering to a budget can be challenging due to the discipline required and the emotional triggers that can lead to overspending or misusing savings. Successful budgeting involves viewing financial discipline as a pathway to freedom rather than a restriction.

For example, the temptation to use emergency funds for non-emergencies often arises from poor financial planning and immediate desires. A well-thought-out budget helps avoid such impulsive decisions, protecting your long-term financial health.

One fundamental principle of sound financial management is to keep funds within their designated "boxes." Do not use money from one box (like your emergency fund) for another purpose (like leisure spending). This ensures that each part of your budget fulfills its intended role without compromising others.

Each financial box serves a distinct purpose: your emergency fund is for unexpected critical needs, while discretionary spending should cover non-essentials that enhance your lifestyle. Misusing these funds can leave you vulnerable in actual emergencies.

For instance, using emergency funds for an impulsive purchase might seem harmless, but if a true emergency arises shortly after, you might not have enough funds and could end up in debt. Such short-term decisions can lead to long-term financial problems.

To maintain financial health, it's crucial to respect the boundaries set for each fund or account. Each should have a clear purpose, whether for emergencies, retirement, or vacations, and you should stick to these designated roles to avoid potential financial difficulties.

Using a Budget to Strengthen Financial Discipline

Budgeting is an excellent tool for enhancing financial discipline. By establishing spending and saving limits, you develop the mental strength needed to adhere to your financial goals. It's challenging to resist temptations, but a budget provides a clear path to follow, guiding you through tough times.

Sticking to a budget can be compared to muscle training; consistent practice makes you stronger. Over time, the satisfaction of adhering to a budget surpasses the fleeting joy of impulsive spending. This shift in mindset transforms budgeting from a tedious task to a powerful, empowering habit.

Here are strategies to maintain financial discipline:

1. **Set Clear Rules:** Clearly define when to use your emergency fund. Suitable scenarios may include life-threatening situations, critical healthcare needs, or severe, unexpected events like job loss. Avoid using these funds for other purposes.
2. **Automate Your Savings:** Automation can help structure your finances. Set up automatic transfers to your emergency and other savings accounts to help them grow steadily and reduce the temptation to use these funds frivolously.
3. **Create a Separate Fund for Wants:** In addition to an emergency fund, establish a savings account for discretionary spending. This could be for luxuries, hobbies, or vacations. Dedicated accounts help prevent the misuse of funds earmarked for emergencies.
4. **Exercise Patience:** Resist the urge for immediate gratification. Delaying purchases until you've saved for them not only protects your emergency fund but also enhances the enjoyment of your purchases, knowing they were well-planned and budgeted for.

Cross-utilizing funds can create future problems, offering temporary satisfaction that could lead to significant stress during actual emergencies. Maintaining distinct financial "boxes" ensures that you are well-prepared for any situation without compromising your stability.

As my financial independence grew, I continued to budget meticulously. Despite having more disposable income, I adhered to the principles of wise saving and spending. These values are something I impart to my son, reflecting the teachings of my father. Despite his school environment at Oakridge International School—where wealth and luxury are commonplace—my son remains unswayed by ostentation. He values authenticity and practicality, often opting for public transportation over more lavish modes. This preference is a testament to the values I've instilled in him, demonstrating a thoughtful approach to wealth and its display.

Budgeting for Long-Term Financial Health

Money not only serves a practical purpose but also reveals much about a person's character, particularly in how they support others. When someone readily says, "I'll give it to you, don't worry," it demonstrates their willingness to help. In contrast, excuses like, "Nahi yaar, abhi nahi hai" (No, not right now) quickly show their real priorities.

These instances aren't merely about financial assistance; they reveal how much individuals value relationships. Money offers profound insights into human behavior. Whether it's lending ₹5,000 or providing support during tough times, these small gestures profoundly indicate someone's true priorities.

True worth isn't measured by material possessions but by how individuals manage their money and support others. While superficial judgments based on cars, clothes, or lifestyle are common, it's the subtle acts of financial assistance that truly reveal one's character.

The primary aim of budgeting isn't just to scrape by day-to-day but to ensure long-term financial health. An effective budget allows for a comfortable present while securing a stable future. For me, budgeting means balancing—saving for emergencies, investing wisely, and enjoying the present.

Budgeting requires adopting a long-term view of finances, aligning with broader principles of mindful money management. Each rupee allocated should advance your financial goals, covering immediate needs, future security, or fulfilling a larger life purpose. It's about more than just survival; it's about flourishing in the future.

Budgeting as a Reflection of Your Financial Psychology

I've discovered that money is not just a means to satisfy needs or desires; it's a reflection of a person's character. My close circle of friends, who offer support without hesitation, exemplifies this. When I lend money, I do so with the understanding that it may not be returned, and that's okay because it reflects genuine friendship and mutual support.

However, not everyone views money similarly. My observations of the "psychology of money" reveal that many people, despite their outward wealth, are often reluctant to share it. It seems their possessions are more for show than for aiding others. Hesitation to lend even small amounts often exposes a person's real priorities and values. These interactions have taught me that money's essence isn't about accumulating wealth or displaying it but about managing it responsibly and using it to support oneself and others.

At the core of these reflections is a vital truth: **It's not about how much money you make but how you manage it.** Effective money management involves setting aside funds for emergencies, investing for the future, or budgeting for acts of generosity. The real value of money comes from its thoughtful allocation and use.

Through budgeting, I've aligned my finances with my values. A well-crafted budget is more than just numbers; it's a life roadmap, ensuring comfort now and security later. It directs every rupee toward significant goals, be they personal, financial, or communal, and allows space for generosity without compromising my financial security.

In This Chapter...

Success isn't measured by wealth or luxurious possessions but by the decisions made with available resources. Money reveals our deepest values and our handling of it speaks volumes about our character. I manage my finances in a way that reflects what I value most—family, friends, financial security, and helping others. And that, to me, is the true definition of success.

*"WEALTH IS NOT ABOUT
HAVING A LOT OF MONEY; IT'S
ABOUT HAVING A LOT OF
OPTIONS."*

— *Chris Rock*

₹4
SAVING MONEY
WITHOUT SACRIFICING
DESIRES

FAQ

Q: Do you follow anyone's philosophy when it comes to managing money?

I follow myself—my own experiences, and, at times, my mistakes. Every misstep taught me a lesson. Over time, I began observing the financial discipline of my elders, adapting their approaches to create a system that works in daily life. I've essentially crafted my own path based on trial, error, and a focus on smart money habits.

"A penny saved, is a penny earned."

–Benjamin Franklin, American Polymath

In today's fast-paced world, balancing the need to save money while fulfilling our desires often feels overwhelming. Many people struggle with the belief that saving means giving up what they love most—enjoying delicious meals at restaurants, traveling to new destinations, or indulging in hobbies that bring joy and creativity to their lives. This perception can create a mental block, leading to feelings of deprivation and frustration.

However, embracing a mindset focused on financial wellness allows us to pursue our passions while making thoughtful, intentional financial decisions. Imagine a life where you can fully enjoy your favorite activities, treat yourself to occasional luxuries, and still build a strong savings account for future goals. This ideal lifestyle is not a distant dream but a tangible reality achievable through smart spending strategies.

This chapter is about saving money without sacrificing the things that make you happy. We will explore practical strategies for reducing everyday expenses while still enjoying life's pleasures. The key to this approach is 'smart spending,' a concept that helps you balance your desires with your financial goals.

Understanding that you can lead a fulfilling life while building a healthy savings account is essential. This chapter will provide actionable strategies and mindset shifts that empower you to save money without compromising the experiences and pleasures that make life truly enjoyable. By adopting a balanced approach to your finances, you can confidently work toward your goals while continuing to enjoy the joys of living fully.

Let's explore how to enhance your financial wellness without giving up the things you love. Through mindful choices and innovative spending habits, you can create a lifestyle that celebrates your passions and aspirations.

Understanding Financial Strategies for Saving

Planning for the Future

Effective financial management starts with forward-thinking planning. By visualizing your future goals—whether it's owning your dream home, traveling the world, or investing in your education—you can create a structured approach to your finances. This helps you focus on what truly matters and guides your financial decisions with intention.

Creating a Vision for Your Future

Start by envisioning the life you want to lead. Take a moment to imagine where you see yourself in five, ten, or even twenty years:

- Are you relaxing on a beach during your annual vacation?
- Do you own a cozy home with a garden?
- Are you pursuing a career that aligns with your passions?

This mental exercise is important because it forms the foundation for setting concrete financial goals.

Setting Clear Goals

Once you have a vision, it's time to turn that vision into clear financial goals. Setting specific goals is crucial in your journey toward financial wellness. Begin by categorizing your goals into short-term and long-term ones. Short-term goals might include saving for a vacation or paying off a small debt, while long-term goals could involve saving for retirement or buying a house.

Here's a practical exercise: Take a piece of paper and create two columns—one for short-term goals and one for long-term goals. Under each category, write down specific objectives, target amounts, and timelines. For example:

- **Short-term Goals:**
  - Save ₹1,65,000 for a vacation by next year.
  - Pay off ₹1,25,000 of credit card debt within six months.

- **Long-term Goals:**
  - ○ Save ₹40,00,000 for a down payment on a house in five years.
  - ○ Build a retirement fund of ₹4,00,00,000 by age 60.

Understanding the Financial Implications

After you've listed your goals, the next step is to understand the financial implications of each. This brings clarity, allowing you to calculate how much you need to save regularly to reach your targets. For instance, if you want to save ₹40,00,000 for a home in five years, you'll need to save around ₹66,667 each month.

Creating a Budget that Aligns with Your Goals

Now that you have clear goals and savings amounts, the next step is to create a budget that supports these objectives. This means tracking your income and expenses, identifying areas where you can cut back, and redirecting those funds to savings. For example, if you spend a lot on dining out, consider reducing restaurant visits to once a week and using the extra money for your savings.

Staying Flexible and Revising Your Plans

Life is unpredictable, and your circumstances may change. That's why it's important to stay flexible and revisit your financial plans regularly. Set aside time, maybe quarterly or bi-annually, to review your goals and track your progress. If your financial situation improves or new opportunities arise, don't hesitate to adjust your goals to reflect these changes.

Embracing the Journey

Financial planning is not just about reaching your goals but about enjoying the process along the way. As you work toward your financial objectives, remember to celebrate the small wins. Whether it's reaching a savings milestone or successfully sticking to your budget for a month, these moments of success will help keep you motivated and focused on your financial journey.

By embracing forward-thinking planning, setting clear goals, and staying flexible, you can build a financially stable future that allows you to pursue your desires without sacrificing your savings. This approach not only helps you achieve your dreams but also gives you confidence and control over your financial life.

Understanding Desires vs. Needs

Finding the right balance between saving and spending starts with understanding the difference between our desires and our needs. While this distinction might seem simple at first, it plays a key role in managing our finances effectively.

Our needs include essential things like food, shelter, healthcare, and education, which are critical for our well-being and survival. Desires, on the other hand, refer to things we want for pleasure, enjoyment, or self-expression—like luxury items, entertainment, or unique experiences.

Psychologically, desires can have a powerful influence on our spending behavior. For example, marketing often targets our desires, creating a sense of urgency to buy the latest gadget or trend. Being aware of this distinction helps us prioritize our spending and make more mindful financial decisions.

Consider this scenario: you've been dreaming about owning a luxury car for months. It's not a necessity, but the desire is strong. By recognizing it as a desire rather than a need, you can assess whether this purchase aligns with your long-term financial goals.

Defining Needs and Desires

Needs are the essentials required for our survival and overall well-being. These include necessities such as food, shelter, healthcare, and education. They form the foundation of our daily lives and are critical for both physical and mental health. For example, without access to nutritious food, adequate housing, or necessary medical care, our quality of life would rapidly deteriorate.

In contrast, desires refer to what we crave for enjoyment, pleasure, and self-expression. These can include luxury items, entertainment, hobbies, and unique experiences that enhance our lives but are not essential for survival. While desires can enrich our lives and provide fulfillment, they can also lead to impulsive spending if not managed carefully.

The Psychological Influence of Desires

Psychologically, our desires can have a powerful impact on our spending habits. Marketing and advertising often take advantage of these desires, creating a sense of urgency to acquire the latest gadget, fashion item, or experience. This urgency can cloud our judgment, leading to impulsive purchases that may not align with our financial goals. Recognizing the role desires play in decision-making can help us navigate these influences more effectively.

Prioritizing Spending

Understanding the difference between needs and desires is essential for prioritizing our spending. When faced with financial decisions, it's helpful to ask ourselves critical questions: Is this purchase essential for my well-being? Does it contribute to my long-term goals? By evaluating our desires in the context of our needs, we can make more conscious financial choices that align with our values and objectives.

Evaluating a Purchase

Consider this scenario: you've been eyeing a designer handbag for months. The desire for this handbag feels compelling, especially when you see it featured on social media or in a luxury store. However, recognizing this as a desire rather than a need allows you to evaluate it more thoughtfully. Ask yourself:

- Is this handbag essential for my daily life or well-being?
- Will this purchase positively impact my financial situation in the long term?
- Are there alternatives that can fulfill my desire without compromising my budget?

By engaging in this reflective process, you can better assess whether the purchase aligns with your financial goals and whether it's worth the investment.

Distinguishing Needs and Desires

Distinguishing between needs and desires is an essential step toward achieving financial wellness. By understanding this distinction, you can prioritize your spending, resist impulsive purchases driven by temporary desires, and ultimately create a more balanced financial life. This awareness empowers you to make informed choices that align with your immediate needs and long-term aspirations, allowing you to enjoy life's pleasures while maintaining a healthy savings account.

The Mindset Shift

Shifting our mindset about money is crucial for achieving financial balance. Many people view money as a limited resource, which leads to feelings of deprivation. Instead, it's important to see money as a tool for creating opportunities and enjoying life.

Techniques for reframing our thoughts about spending and saving include practicing gratitude for what we already have and focusing on experiences rather than material possessions. For example, view a trip with friends as an opportunity to bond and create memories rather than seeing it as a financial burden. This shift in perspective can lead to healthier spending habits.

A friend of mine adopted a mindset transformation, shifting from a scarcity mindset to one of abundance. This change led to more mindful spending and, ultimately, greater joy in their financial decisions. Let's explore how we can make the same shift. The following insights address common challenges people face when managing their finances, particularly regarding spending habits, and highlight the difference between intentional spending and waste. Here's a summary of the key points:

1. **Spending vs. Wasting**: Think about shopping for one item but ending up with several. This is often due to a lack of control. However, it's crucial to learn how to restrain spending. Life teaches us these lessons naturally—when we realize we've spent money on unnecessary things while neglecting important needs.

2. **Budgeting Strategies**: Budgeting involves setting money aside into "boxes" (both figurative and literal) and using it only for urgent needs. Having a plan is key to avoiding overspending. Those who don't adopt such strategies often return to them after making financial mistakes.

3. **The Concept of Moderation**: This is especially relevant during festive seasons like Diwali when people often buy clothes for special occasions that are rarely worn again. This represents a broader cultural habit of accumulating possessions with the mindset of "it might be useful later," only for those items to sit idle.

4. **Mindful Consumption**: Consider meal portions before ordering food when dining out to prevent waste. This habit connects to being conscious of how much we truly need versus over-ordering simply because we can afford it. There's also a noticeable difference in how money spent with family (intentional and valuable) contrasts with spending with friends (often wasteful due to a lack of planning).

5. **Clothing and Materialism**: Many of us own far more clothes than we need, especially in the corporate world, where there's pressure to maintain a fresh wardrobe every day or week. This habit is unnecessary, and I encourage repeating clothes for special occasions like Diwali instead of succumbing *(dic. meaning: failing to resist temptation)* to societal pressures.

6. **Social Media Influence**: Social media has amplified the pressure to constantly appear fresh and new, especially regarding what others are wearing. This mindset fosters waste. We should resist allowing social media to dictate our financial choices.

Case Study: Planning for a Car Purchase
The 4-Year Strategy

To demonstrate the power of careful planning, let's look at Mina's story of purchasing a car. Mina, a young professional, dreamed of owning a brand-new Mercedes. Instead of impulsively buying it on credit, she created a four-year savings plan. By setting aside a specific percentage of her monthly income, she gradually accumulated enough money to purchase the car outright. This approach built anticipation and excitement as she worked towards her goal.

Double Goals: Buying Two Cars

Life often presents unexpected desires. In Mina's case, halfway through her savings journey, she realized she wanted two cars: a compact car for city driving and an SUV for family outings. This revelation could have derailed her original savings plan. However, she reassessed her priorities, adjusted her budget, and extended her savings timeline. In the end, she successfully achieved both goals without sacrificing her financial stability.

The Role of Patience in Financial Success Patience plays a crucial role in financial success. Delaying gratification often leads to greater satisfaction when you finally make that purchase. For example, rather than giving in to the urge to buy a luxury item on credit, waiting and saving for it can result in a more rewarding and meaningful experience when the purchase is made. The sense of accomplishment that comes from reaching your financial goal is truly invaluable.

This case study highlights that financial discipline is a gradual process. While spending isn't inherently bad, it should be intentional and aligned with your personal values and long-term goals.

Setting Financial Goals

Defining clear financial goals is essential for aligning your desires with your financial plans. Begin by reflecting on what you truly want to achieve, both in the short and long term. Are you saving for a dream vacation, a new car, or a home? Once you have your goals set, break them down into actionable steps.

For example, if your goal is to travel, research the cost of your desired destination and create a savings plan accordingly.

Creating a Balanced Budget

This has already been discussed in a previous chapter. A balanced budget is the cornerstone of financial health. To create one that allows for both saving and indulging in desires, follow these steps:

1. **Assess Your Income and Expenses:** Start by tracking your monthly income and expenses. Categorize your spending into needs, desires, and savings.
2. **Set Clear Financial Goals:** Define your short-term and long-term goals. These can range from saving for a vacation to building an emergency fund.
3. **Allocate Funds Wisely:** Divide your income into categories, ensuring you allocate a portion for savings while still setting aside funds for your desires.
4. **Review and Adjust Regularly:** Life is dynamic, so it's essential to review and adjust your budget periodically.

Tools like budgeting apps can simplify this process, offering insights into spending habits and helping you stay accountable.

Finding Joy in Savings: Contrary to popular belief, saving money can be a source of joy rather than deprivation. When you view saving as a means to achieve your desires, your perspective changes.

Celebrate milestones along your savings journey. Set up small rewards for yourself when you hit certain savings goals—this could be as simple as a day out with friends or treating yourself to a nice coffee.

The psychological benefits of saving are significant. Knowing you have a financial cushion can reduce anxiety and create a sense of security. This, in turn, allows you to enjoy life more fully, knowing you're working toward your goals.

Smart Savings and Investments

The journey of saving money without sacrificing your desires is not just about strict budgeting or depriving yourself. It's about cultivating a mindset that values both saving and enjoying life. You can find harmony in your financial journey by understanding the distinction between needs and desires, shifting your mindset, creating a balanced budget, and setting clear financial goals.

Using Savings to Pay EMIs

One strategy to consider is using your savings to cover monthly car loan payments (EMIs). This approach involves saving enough over time so that the interest earned from investments can cover these payments. This way, you preserve your principal investment while enjoying the benefits of ownership without the stress of debt.

The Power of Fixed Deposits and Interest

A fixed deposit account can act as a safety net for future expenses, including EMIs. This method allows your money to grow through interest, providing you with a more substantial financial cushion. Imagine setting up a fixed deposit specifically earmarked for your future car payments. This way, you can enjoy the benefits of ownership while maintaining your overall financial health.

The Psychological and Emotional Side of Financial Planning
Low-Risk vs. High-Risk Investments

Understanding different investment strategies is essential when planning for future financial goals. There are various options, ranging from low-risk investments like bonds and savings accounts to higher-risk choices such as stocks and mutual funds. Each type of investment offers a different risk-reward balance. Depending on your comfort level with risk and your financial objectives, you can adjust your investment strategy to meet your needs.

Managing Risk in Personal Investments

When it comes to investments, it's important to approach them with a safety-first mentality. This means protecting your principal amount while allowing for growth. One way to manage risk is by diversifying your investments. By spreading your money across different assets, you reduce the risk of a downturn in any one area. Regularly reviewing and adjusting your investment portfolio based on your financial situation can help you stay on track with your goals.

The Satisfaction of Smart Spending

One of the greatest rewards of financial planning is the emotional benefit it provides. When you make wise spending choices—whether it's for a vacation, a new gadget, or a dining experience—you enhance the joy of ownership. This satisfaction is even greater when you know your financial plan is solid. It turns spending from a source of stress into a rewarding experience that reflects your values.

Delayed Gratification and Financial Patience

Delayed gratification is a powerful principle in personal finance. Waiting to make a purchase can often be more satisfying than giving in to the urge for instant gratification. When you take the time to save for something you really want, it builds anticipation and excitement. This shift from impulsive buying to thoughtful saving leads to better financial health and deeper satisfaction when you finally make the purchase.

Smart Spending Strategies

Prioritizing desires while maintaining financial responsibility requires smart spending strategies. Here are some effective approaches:

- **Delayed Gratification:** Instead of making impulse purchases, practice delaying them. Give yourself a set period to think about the purchase. Often, the desire will fade, and you'll save money.

- **Prioritize Experiences:** Research shows that spending money on experiences—like travel or concerts—brings more lasting happiness than material possessions. By prioritizing experiences, you can enjoy your desires while being financially responsible.

- **Seek Alternatives:** Look for less expensive ways to fulfill your desires. For example, instead of dining out at a high-end restaurant, try cooking a new recipe at home or hosting a potluck with friends.

Let's dive deeper into mindful saving, spending, and financial planning. Here's a breakdown of the key concepts:

1. **Mindful Saving vs. Mindless Saving:** It's important to save mindfully for planned future needs rather than hoarding money without purpose. Saving should act as a safety net for tough times, but it's crucial to use that money wisely for future expenses.

2. **The Unpredictability of Life:** Events like demonetization and COVID-19 show how unexpected circumstances can catch people off guard, especially when they haven't planned financially.

3. **The Consequences of Poor Financial Planning:** The struggles during COVID-19 and demonetization highlight how those without financial planning suffered, while those who had saved and invested wisely were better prepared for the challenges.

4. **Multiple Streams of Income:** Diversifying income sources is a wise strategy. People with side businesses, such as cloud

kitchens or online stores, were able to sustain themselves during the pandemic.

5. **Intergenerational Lessons on Money:** Parents often emphasize saving, but now, in hindsight, they appreciate the importance of mindful saving and spending. It's important for parents to teach their children not only the importance of saving but also the reasoning behind it.

6. **Money Habits are Addictive:** Spending money can become addictive, just like any other vice. Learning to manage money effectively is crucial for ensuring long-term financial security.

7. **Practical Advice:** Some practical strategies for managing money include keeping cash out of sight to avoid temptation and focusing on fulfilling needs before wants. This careful, strategic handling of money leads to long-term security and peace of mind.

A Holistic Approach to Wants and Needs

Creating a "Want Box"

To manage your desires effectively, consider setting up a "want box." This concept involves designating funds specifically for indulgences. By saving intentionally for your wants, you can enjoy them without guilt. It turns your desires into achievable goals, allowing you to fully enjoy the experience when the time is right. This box also serves as a tangible reminder of your achievements and the joy of fulfilling your desires.

Knowing When to Spend

Deciding when to make a purchase requires thoughtful reflection. Asking yourself a few critical questions can clarify your motivations and help you align your purchases with your financial reality:

- "Should I buy this?"
- "Can I afford it?"

- "Why do I want to buy this?"

This thought process helps you evaluate the value of your desires against your financial situation. Making purchases based on careful consideration rather than impulse leads to more fulfilling and rewarding experiences.

In This Chapter...

We learned that strategic financial planning is crucial for achieving your desires without compromising your future. By thoughtfully planning your purchases, setting clear goals, and managing your finances wisely, you can create a fulfilling life where your desires are met while ensuring your savings stay intact. The key takeaway is that saving does not mean deprivation—it enhances your experiences and enriches your financial journey.

Embrace patience, celebrate your progress, and remember that the journey toward financial freedom is just as rewarding as reaching the destination.

Each person's path to financial wellness is unique. It's about discovering what works best for you and finding joy in both saving and enjoying the experiences that enrich your life. So, take that first step today—embrace the balance of saving and living well!

"BEWARE OF LITTLE EXPENSES. A SMALL LEAK WILL SINK A GREAT SHIP."

— *Benjamin Franklin*

₹5
THE CONCEPT OF MONEY BOXES

FAQ

Q: Why is money management important to you, even though you're financially well-off?

I follow myself—my own experiences, and, at times, my mistakes. Every misstep taught me a lesson. Over time, I began observing the financial discipline of my elders, adapting their approaches to create a system that works in daily life. I've essentially crafted my own path based on trial, error, and a focus on smart money habits.

"Too many people spend money they haven't earned to buy things they don't want to impress people they don't like."

–Will Rogers, Humorist and Entertainer

In today's ever-evolving consumer-driven world, we are constantly bombarded with messages urging us to spend. From billboards to social media, it often seems like the more you own, the more successful you are. However, true financial wisdom isn't about accumulating things. It's about adopting a disciplined approach to earning, saving, and spending wisely. This chapter will explore the philosophy of valuing your money—learning to appreciate every penny you earn and understanding the broader impact of your spending habits.

Whether you're starting your career or have been working for years, mastering effective financial management is key to achieving long-term stability and peace of mind. One powerful approach to money management is the concept of money boxes.

This chapter delves into money boxes—how they work and how they can help you achieve your financial goals while securing your future. The concept is simple but transformative: by categorizing your money into distinct "boxes," you can build a healthier, more intentional relationship with your finances.

Imagine having dedicated funds for different financial goals— vacations, emergency savings, gifts, or investments. This organizational strategy not only brings clarity and control but also fosters a proactive mindset for managing your money.

Prioritizing Your Goals Over Social Expectations

The pressure to "keep up" with others is strong. We often feel the urge to match our peers, whether through clothing, cars, or homes. A close friend once told me, "At least buy a car now! Look at everyone around you!" I had just completed a big business deal, and for outsiders, it might have seemed like the perfect time to splurge. But buying a car was never a priority for me.

Owning a car wasn't high on my list of financial goals. It wasn't that I couldn't afford it, but I valued the things that truly brought happiness and fulfillment. A new car might offer short-term joy but wouldn't contribute to my long-term financial well-being. Instead, I chose to save that money and invest it elsewhere. This decision, made in a moment, has paid off over the years—not only financially but also in terms of peace of mind.

This choice reflects my broader philosophy: simplicity over extravagance. I wear a small rotation of 10-12 outfits at the office, and for social events, I have just a few outfits that I don't often wear. Even for important family occasions, I rarely buy new clothes. Recently, my wife jokingly pointed out that I'd worn the same suit to several weddings. "You're going to wear that again?" she asked. My response: "Why not?" I might change the shirt, but that suit is making another appearance.

This isn't about depriving myself; it's about making conscious, thoughtful decisions. Simplicity doesn't mean living without desires. It means understanding which of your desires are truly important and distinguishing between wants and needs. When you prioritize long-term financial goals over temporary social expectations, you begin to make decisions that benefit your future.

Manifesting Financial Prosperity

A core principle of my financial philosophy is the belief that money is more than just a resource—it's a companion that thrives in an atmosphere of care and respect. I often tell my friends, "Money is my best friend. Money loves me." I repeat this affirmation daily to strengthen my connection with financial prosperity.

When I observe my friends' financial habits, I notice a stark contrast. Despite earning similar incomes, their approaches to money differ greatly. Many are trapped in a cycle of spending, constantly chasing immediate gratification. This is a reminder that financial discipline is not just an idea but a way of life that must be learned and practiced.

In today's digital world, it's important to remember the lessons we were taught from an early age. While digital money and online transactions make things easier, they can also blur our sense of the true value of money. When we physically hold cash, we create a tangible connection to it, making it easier to understand its worth and manage it wisely.

The Power of Community and Shared Experiences

The company we keep has a significant influence on our financial habits. Looking back on my journey, I realize that the friends I surrounded myself with played a key role in reinforcing the values I learned at home. We shared experiences, stories, and lessons about financial responsibility, which helped keep us on track.

We often discussed the intricacies of money management, exchanging tips and advice to improve our financial decisions. We understood the importance of living within our means and making informed choices. This collective approach to financial responsibility became our guiding light, protecting us from the dangers of reckless spending.

The Thrill of Saving

When you begin saving money, a sense of thrill accompanies the journey. It's more than just increasing the numbers in your bank account—it's about the security and confidence that comes with having a financial cushion. I often tell my friends that once you accumulate your "money boxes"—whether literal or metaphorical—you feel an empowering surge. Yes, I'm wealthy, I think, but it's not just about the money—it's the peace of mind that comes from managing it wisely.

Case Study: Real-Life Transformations

Let me share Ricky's story, which beautifully illustrates the power of financial discipline. Ricky is a photographer with a passion for writing a book. Full of ideas and enthusiasm, he often finds himself overwhelmed by credit card bills and stress, which drain his creativity.

One evening, as we were discussing our financial habits, I encouraged Ricky to take a closer look at his spending patterns. At first, he was skeptical. "How can I change my spending habits?" he asked. But I assured him that change was possible. I introduced him to my "box concept" and showed him how he could apply it to his own situation.

Ricky decided to track his spending, categorizing his expenses into needs and wants. He was shocked to see how much he was spending on unnecessary outings, often overindulging at restaurants and bars. Together, we set a specific budget for dining out, and he committed to sticking to it.

Just a few months later, Ricky's approach had completely transformed. He reported back to me, beaming with pride. "Anand, you were right! By cutting back on eating out, I saved money to invest in my photography gear. I'm also putting aside money for the book I want to write!"

That moment marked a turning point in Ricky's life. He discovered that financial discipline didn't just result in savings; it sparked joy and creativity. As his "boxes" grew fuller each month, he felt liberated from financial anxiety and more empowered to pursue his passions.

The Philosophy of Money Management

Whenever I'm sitting with friends, I often hear them share stories about their financial journeys. One evening, after a night of cards during Diwali, Ricky leaned in and asked me how I manage my finances so effortlessly. I told him, "There's no secret; just certain rules I follow." This piqued his interest. He asked, "What are these rules? How can they be applied?"

I explained my philosophy: I've created "boxes" in my life. Each box represents a specific category of spending and saving. Everyone has needs, wants, and desires, but the key is allocating money wisely across these boxes. I maintain a set amount for my regular lifestyle that covers my basic needs, while another box is dedicated to my aspirations, such as travel or special purchases.

The key is discipline—resisting the urge to dip into those boxes for anything unnecessary. By prioritizing saving over spontaneous spending, I've found myself more grounded, focused, and ultimately fulfilled.

Discipline Leads to Happiness

Discipline is a recurring theme in my financial philosophy. It's an essential part of managing money well. Ricky isn't the only one who has benefited from this approach; I've seen countless others reap the rewards of fiscal discipline.

One such person is my friend Shaji, who sought advice on managing his spending habits. Before implementing the box concept, Shaji often spent impulsively, leaving him feeling anxious about his finances. He came to me one day, expressing concern about his monthly expenses and a desire to save.

"Anand," he said, "I feel like I'm living paycheck to paycheck. I want to break this cycle, but I don't know how."

I suggested he apply the same principles I had shared with Ricky. We created a plan that involved categorizing his expenses into boxes—one for necessities, another for savings, and a third for entertainment. The idea was to prioritize saving while still enjoying life but without overspending.

Shaji followed the plan with determination. He made small changes, like cooking at home and limiting outings. Over time, he began to see tangible results. "I can't believe it!" he exclaimed. "I saved 30,000 rupees this month just by being mindful of my spending. I didn't even miss those outings."

By focusing on his boxes, Shaji gained a renewed sense of control over his life. He no longer felt trapped by his finances; instead, he was empowered to make choices aligned with his goals.

The Psychological Shift

When you embrace saving, the mental shift is profound—it becomes almost addictive. It's hard to go back to your old spending habits once you start witnessing the benefits of saving—seeing those boxes grow and the money accumulate.

One evening, a friend confided in me about his struggles with partying. He had been spending large sums every week on nights out with friends. "I can't keep up with this," he admitted. "It feels like I'm throwing money away."

I suggested a radical approach: take a month off from partying. He was skeptical but agreed to try it for two months. "Just think about what you could save," I urged him. "Every weekend you don't go out could save you 20,000 rupees."

He took my advice to heart. Ultimately, he saved over 1.5 lakhs by cutting back on his nights out. When he shared his experience with me, I could see the shift in his mindset. "I didn't realize how much those outings cost me," he said. "Now, I'm saving money for things that really matter."

This transformation demonstrates how powerful the concept of saving can be. It changes your perspective on money and how you choose to spend it. The feeling of having money saved—knowing that it's available for something meaningful—can shift your entire outlook on life.

The Community Effect

Saving money is not just an individual journey; it has a ripple effect that can influence those around you. As I've shared my insights with friends, I've seen how they've been inspired to adopt similar practices. It creates a beautiful cycle of financial empowerment.

One day, while discussing my savings approach with friends, I noticed one of them, Vikram, nodding along. "You know," he said, "I've always been skeptical about saving. I thought it was boring. But seeing the changes in you guys has motivated me."

Vikram decided to try a similar strategy. He started small, putting aside a portion of his salary each month. Before he knew it, he was sharing his success with others, and a community around saving began to form.

A powerful dynamic emerged as people discussed their successes and challenges. "I saved 10,000 rupees last month just by cutting down on impulse buys," one friend shared. "It's amazing how much money you can save when you understand your spending habits!"

The more we talked, the more we inspired each other. This camaraderie fostered accountability and a sense of collective growth. As each person experienced their own financial transformation, they became advocates for saving, encouraging others to join the movement.

The Long-Term Vision

At its core, saving is about foresight—understanding that every small decision today can lead to a more secure future. I often remind my friends that saving isn't just about accumulating wealth; it's about setting yourself up for success in the long run.

As I explained to Ricky, planning isn't just about the present; it's about envisioning where you want to be in three to five years and creating a roadmap. I often reflect on my own journey—how I learned to allocate my resources wisely and the discipline that came with it.

Every time I save more, I imagine what I can achieve. Whether it's traveling to new destinations or investing in my personal growth, the anticipation of those future experiences fuels my desire to save.

In our conversations, we often share how our savings have allowed us to embrace opportunities we once thought were out of reach. One friend recently used his savings to attend a photography workshop abroad, and another invested in a startup that aligned with their passion.

Realizing that saving is an enabler of dreams makes the practice so powerful. It's not just about denying ourselves small pleasures; it's about choosing to invest in our futures.

The Joy of Giving

Beyond personal gain, saving also opens doors to generosity. As we save and grow our financial base, we find ourselves able to give back to our communities and support causes that matter to us.

One of the most rewarding aspects of saving money is the ability to share that wealth with others. Whether donating to a charity or helping a friend in need, the joy of giving is amplified when you know you have the financial means.

Ricky, for instance, recently shared his desire to contribute to a local initiative supporting underprivileged children. "I wouldn't have thought about this a year ago," he said. "But now that I've been saving, I feel like I can make a difference."

Your Behavior Shapes the Next Generation

The habits you practice today will likely be passed down to your children. This realization has shaped my approach to finances. If I am careless with money, my son will likely follow in my footsteps. But if I demonstrate financial discipline, he will absorb that lesson naturally. Children learn through observation, and the financial choices we make are not only personal but also educational.

For example, I've taught my son the importance of living within one's means. He has seen me practice restraint—whether in buying new gadgets, clothes, or a car—and he's starting to understand that simplicity and frugality are not constraints. They are freedoms. When you have control over your finances, you gain the freedom to make more meaningful life decisions in the future.

Financial discipline isn't just about saving for your own security; it's about setting an example that will shape the financial behaviors of future generations. If you normalize excessive spending or reckless financial behavior, you set a dangerous precedent. However, if you emphasize saving, budgeting, and responsible spending, you provide your children with a foundation for long-term financial health.

The Role of Family in Financial Education

The lessons my father taught me remain etched in my memory. I remember preparing for my cousin's wedding, feeling excited about buying new clothes. My father, however, insisted on budgeting. "Tell me how much everything will cost, and don't exceed that budget," he said. It was a valuable lesson that emphasized the importance of financial planning.

At that moment, I realized the significance of distinguishing between needs and wants. I presented him with a budget of 10,000 rupees, which included a few extra items I felt were necessary. Instead of simply giving me money, he gave me an opportunity to reflect on my choices. This taught me that every financial decision matters.

Through these experiences, my father instilled the importance of accountability in financial matters. "Once this money leaves your hand, it's gone," he reminded me. His words have echoed in my mind, encouraging me to value every rupee. This foundation has played a key role in shaping my perspective on money and responsibility.

As I reflect on these lessons, I realize that parenting plays an essential role in shaping financial habits. Children who grow up without guidance may struggle with money management as adults. The values instilled during childhood create the framework for how one approaches money—whether they prioritize savings, investment, or impulsive spending.

The Importance of Delayed Gratification

The principle of delayed gratification lies at the heart of financial discipline. In a world that encourages instant gratification, where we often want everything right now, mastering patience can be the key to long-term financial success. For example, consider the difference between impulsively buying the latest smartphone and waiting until you've saved enough to purchase it without straining your budget. In the first scenario, you may feel brief satisfaction, but it's followed by the stress of managing credit card bills or depleting your savings. In the second scenario, you've delayed gratification, but you've gained something far more valuable—financial stability.

This mindset of delayed gratification is crucial when managing your money boxes. You may have a "desire box" for luxury purchases—a car, a vacation, or a designer outfit—but the key is ensuring your necessities are met first. The beauty of this system is that it allows you to indulge in your desires only after your needs and long-term goals are taken care of. You don't have to deny yourself the things you love—you just have to earn them.

The Money Box Concept: Harboring Financial Discipline

One of the most powerful tools I've used in my financial journey is the concept of "money boxes." This simple yet effective method has helped me compartmentalize my finances, ensuring that my spending aligns with my goals. The idea is to create distinct "boxes" or categories for different types of expenses and savings. This approach provides a clear structure for managing your money, making it easier to prioritize needs, save for the future, and indulge in wants without jeopardizing your financial stability.

Imagine two money boxes: transparent boxes for immediate, visible needs and opaque boxes for long-term goals and unseen future requirements. Transparent boxes hold funds for everyday expenses—rent, groceries, utility bills, and basic living costs. Opaque boxes contain savings for larger, long-term goals, such as retirement, your children's education, or a down payment on a house.

This concept works because it forces you to separate your financial needs from your desires. When you have clear boundaries around how much you can spend and save, you're less likely to dip into your future savings to satisfy immediate wants. By doing this, you build a habit of financial discipline that protects your long-term security while still allowing for enjoyment along the way.

Understanding Money Boxes

Money boxes are a straightforward yet effective way to manage your finances. They divide your income into different categories, each assigned a specific purpose. This chapter will introduce the concept of money boxes and explain the steps to create and utilize them effectively.

We'll discuss identifying your financial goals, allocating funds appropriately, and monitoring your progress. By using money boxes, you can take charge of your financial destiny, making informed decisions that align with your values and priorities. This method empowers you to visualize your financial journey, making it easier to navigate challenges and celebrate successes.

Join us as we delve deeper into the transformative power of money boxes, equipping you with the knowledge and tools needed to build a secure financial future. Let's start this journey together.

What Are Money Boxes?

At its core, money boxes divide income into various categories, each serving a specific purpose. Traditionally, we might think of a physical piggy bank or a locked chest of savings. Today, however, these "boxes" can be digital accounts, investments, or savings pots set aside for different goals.

Money boxes aren't just about physically stashing money away. They represent a mindset—a structured, methodical way to handle financial needs, wants, and long-term goals. While many people are familiar with budgeting, money boxes take it one step further by encouraging you to visualize and compartmentalize your finances in a way that is both systematic and empowering.

The History of Money Boxes

The origins of money boxes are rooted in simplicity. For generations, families—especially those led by frugal mothers—relied on physical money boxes or jars to organize funds for specific household needs. One box might be for groceries, another for school fees, and another for saving toward a future purchase. The practice wasn't just about keeping money in check; it was about maintaining a structured way of life that ensured survival during tough times.

This time-tested method evolved over the years, and with the advent of modern banking and financial systems, it's now possible to continue this practice through digital means. Many people today use savings accounts, fixed deposits, or online wallets as modern-day money boxes, making this concept as relevant now as it was decades ago.

Types of Money Boxes

Let's look at the different money boxes you can implement. Each box serves a specific purpose and helps you allocate funds in an organized way, ensuring you meet both your short-term and long-term financial goals.

1. The Needs Box: Covering Daily Essentials

The first and most important box is the **Needs Box**. This is where you store money for your daily essentials—rent or mortgage, groceries, utility bills, and transportation. The idea is simple: set aside a certain amount from each paycheck to cover your basic living expenses.

The beauty of the Needs Box is that it creates predictability in your life. Regularly contributing to this box ensures that your essential needs are always covered, no matter what happens. You'll never have to scramble to pay the rent or feel anxious about making ends meet. A good rule of thumb is to calculate how much you need for your basic expenses and ensure that the amount is consistently placed in your Needs Box before allocating funds to any other area of your life.

2. The Emergency Box: Preparing for the Unexpected

Life is unpredictable, and emergencies can strike when you least expect them—medical bills, home repairs, or job loss. This is where the **Emergency Box** comes in. This box is specifically designed to act as your financial safety net. By setting aside a portion of your monthly income, you build a reserve that can cushion the blow during tough times.

Experts recommend having three to six months' worth of living expenses in this box. The funds in your Emergency Box should only be used when necessary. By having this financial buffer, you reduce stress and gain peace of mind, knowing you are prepared for life's uncertainties.

3. The Wants Box: Pursuing Personal Goals and Desires

After meeting your essential needs and securing your emergency funds, the next step is to create a Wants Box. This is where you set money aside for discretionary spending. Whether upgrading your home, vacationing, or buying a new gadget, the Wants Box allows you to indulge in your desires without feeling guilty or straining your finances.

The key to the Wants Box is moderation. You might allocate a small percentage of your income to this box, gradually building it up until you can afford your next splurge. What's important here is that planning for these expenditures in advance makes you less likely to fall into the trap of impulse spending. When the time comes, you can confidently make your purchase, knowing you've already saved for it.

4. The Asset Box: Investing for the Future

The Asset Box is where you focus on building long-term wealth. Rather than spending your extra cash on depreciating assets (such as cars or electronics), you can use this box to fund investments that will grow in value over time. This might include real estate, stocks, bonds, or a business venture.

Setting specific investment goals is one way to make this box work. For example, you might decide to invest in a property once you've saved enough for a down payment, or you could contribute regularly to a retirement fund. The idea is to turn your money into assets that will generate more wealth for you in the future.

Digital options for your Asset Box, such as Fixed Deposits (FDs), mutual funds, or stock investments, can also be considered here. This is where your financial literacy plays a key role. Making smart, calculated investments ensures your money works for you, providing financial security for years to come.

5. The Lock Box: Safeguarding for Retirement

The Lock Box is a unique money box specifically designed for retirement. Its purpose is to accumulate savings that you won't touch until you're ready to retire. The Lock Box acts as your ultimate financial security blanket. Unlike other boxes that serve more immediate needs or desires, this one is meant to remain untouched for decades.

The beauty of the Lock Box is that it provides you with peace of mind. Knowing that you have substantial savings for your golden years gives you the freedom to live comfortably in the present. By contributing to your Lock Box throughout your working years, you can avoid the common financial struggles many people face in retirement.

This box can be metaphorical—it might represent an investment fund that matures over a long period—or a physical or digital savings account that remains untouched until a specified

---

time. The key here is that discipline and commitment will ensure that you have a stable nest egg when the time comes.

6. Additional Money Boxes to Consider

Once you've established the main boxes for your needs, emergencies, wants, assets, and retirement, you can consider creating additional money boxes for other life goals. For instance:

- **Education Box:** If you plan to return to school or want to save for your children's education, setting aside funds in an Education Box can help you stay on track.
- **Travel Box:** For the globetrotters, having a designated savings box for travel ensures you can enjoy your vacations without dipping into your regular budget.
- **Charity Box:** If giving back is important, having a box dedicated to charitable contributions is a great way to ensure you can consistently donate to causes you care about.

7. Boxes for Different Life Stages

- Financial needs evolve over time, and so should the way you manage your money boxes. The financial responsibilities of a young, single individual differ from those of a family with children, and the approach to budgeting for a single-income household will vary from that of a dual-income one. Understanding these differences allows you to tailor your money boxes to fit your current life stage.

Here's how I recommend structuring your money boxes based on different phases of life:

- **Daily Expenses Box:** This is your most immediate and transparent box, covering everything from rent or mortgage payments to groceries, utilities, and transportation. This box should always be prioritized, regardless of income level or family size. It ensures that your basic living expenses are always covered first.
- **Lifestyle Box:** This box includes spending on non-essential but regular lifestyle expenses, like dining out, entertainment, and hobbies. Budgeting for these extras is important, but keep them separate from your daily needs to avoid overspending. You can

allocate a specific portion of your income for these expenses to ensure they don't overpower other financial goals.

- **Emergency Box:** This box is crucial for unexpected expenses such as medical emergencies, home repairs, or sudden job loss. Financial experts often recommend saving 3 to 6 months of living expenses in this box. It acts as a safety net to reduce financial stress during tough times. Having this box in place gives you peace of mind, knowing you are prepared for life's uncertainties.

- **Future Planning Box:** This box is dedicated to your long-term goals, like saving for your children's education, your retirement, or a future home purchase. The earlier you start filling this box, the more secure your financial future will be. The Future Planning Box ensures you are building towards larger life milestones, even if they seem far off.

- **Desire Box:** This is your luxury fund, reserved for discretionary spending like vacations, a new car, or personal splurges. By keeping this box separate from your daily expenses, you ensure that your desires don't take priority over your needs. This way, you can enjoy life's pleasures without sacrificing financial security.

Psychological Benefits of Money Boxes

Beyond the obvious financial advantages, there are significant psychological benefits to using money boxes. By categorizing your money into specific boxes, you gain control over your finances. This structured approach helps reduce the overwhelm that comes with bills and curbs the temptation of impulse purchases. Setting clear goals for each box creates a sense of accomplishment and progress as you watch your savings grow over time.

Seeing your money accumulate in clear, transparent boxes—whether physical or digital—reinforces good financial habits. It serves as a visual reminder that you're working towards meaningful goals, enhancing your motivation to stick with your plan. This psychological reinforcement is powerful in maintaining financial discipline.

Money Boxes and Financial Generosity

An often-overlooked aspect of financial management is the role of generosity. Including a "Financial Generosity" box in your system allows you to contribute to others without compromising your financial stability. Whether it's supporting a charitable cause, helping a friend in need, or assisting family members, generosity can be an essential part of your financial wellness.

By setting aside funds specifically for giving, you create a habit of generosity that benefits both you and others. This practice fosters a sense of fulfillment, knowing that your financial success is also contributing to making the world a better place. The act of giving, when done consciously and within your means, can enhance your overall sense of financial well-being and peace of mind.

The Philosophy Behind Money Boxes

The concept of money boxes is more than just a budgeting tool; it embodies a philosophy of intentional financial management. By dividing your income into specific categories—such as needs, emergencies, wants, assets, and retirement—you create a structured approach that leads to long-term stability and financial peace of mind.

One pivotal moment in my own journey of financial education occurred when my son, at 17 years old, excitedly shared his understanding of money management. He had earned money from a small business venture and proudly declared, "I take 20% of your profit," with a grin. I realized then that he had already grasped the value of money at such a young age. To him, earning even ₹10,000 or ₹15,000 represented freedom and responsibility.

This essence of financial education is deeply ingrained in families within the Gujarati and Marwari communities. Growing up in such households, children are taught the importance of managing money effectively from a young age. This isn't just a cultural stereotype; it's a guiding principle that has propelled many families to wealth and financial stability. The wisdom passed down through generations emphasizes the value of financial discipline, which ultimately leads to prosperity.

The Dichotomy of Spending

In these communities, the approach to spending can vary dramatically. While some communities may prioritize lavish celebrations and flashy displays of wealth, Gujaratis tend to embrace a more understated lifestyle. Their wealth is often hidden in simplicity, reflecting the belief that true riches do not require outward ostentation.

Instead of spending heavily on material possessions, many Gujaratis and Marwaris invest in experiences. They travel the world, enjoy diverse cultures, and enrich their lives through experiences—maintaining a modest outward appearance. This emphasis on investing in life experiences over material things teaches us an essential lesson: the true value of money lies not in the things it can buy but in the moments and memories it can create.

Reflecting on My Own Upbringing

Reflecting on my upbringing, I realize that my financial education started early. My father played a crucial role in instilling the principles of money management long before I learned about them in school. "Half-day you go to college, and half-day you come to the shop," he instructed me when I was just 16. At the time, I felt a sense of indignation; why should I split my day between education and work?

Yet, in hindsight, this arrangement turned out to be a blessing in disguise. I spent countless hours at the shop, learning the ins and outs of business and finance. With a monthly allowance of 500 rupees, I was responsible for managing my own expenses. If I wanted to indulge in a plate of idli, it came out of my pocket. This small lesson in budgeting taught me a critical skill: the ability to prioritize needs over wants.

Even today, I often reflect on those early experiences. I rarely eat outside, as it's simply a habit ingrained in me from my upbringing. When I find myself at a registration office, I'll often ask the driver to step out, pull out my tiffin box, and enjoy a homemade meal. It's not about the money; it's about discipline. That discipline, which has become second nature, stems from those formative years.

Creating Habits for Financial Wellness

The choices we make today set the tone for our future. Discipline cultivated through careful financial management fosters a mindset that prioritizes savings over impulse spending. When we become accustomed to bringing our meals from home, we develop a habit that extends to our overall financial behaviors. By choosing home-cooked meals, I've discovered not just a way to save money but also a means of cultivating a healthy lifestyle.

Many might question why I opt for home-cooked meals over dining out. The answer lies not just in saving a few rupees but in the psychological understanding that it helps me feel in control of my finances. Each meal represents money spent on groceries; why squander that on outside food? This mindset helps reinforce the values of discipline and prudence—two virtues that have served me well over the years.

To further illustrate this point, I share a story about a friend who struggled with maintaining financial discipline. Initially, we were a group of five close friends, all navigating the transition from school to adulthood. As we stepped into the working world, I found myself dedicating my time to the shop while my friends indulged in a carefree lifestyle. They had wealthy fathers who could afford luxury cars, dining out and extravagant outings. While I respected their choices, I felt no envy. I knew my path would lead to financial stability.

Fast forward to today, and the tables have turned. Many of my friends, despite earning the same amount of money as I did, find themselves perpetually struggling to make ends meet. They spend lavishly and live paycheck to paycheck, their financial habits deeply ingrained over the years. Meanwhile, my disciplined approach has enabled me to save and invest wisely.

It's essential to recognize that financial discipline is not merely a personal journey but a communal effort. The lessons we learn from our families, friends, and communities shape our understanding of money. Through this interplay of experiences, we develop the habits that define our financial lives.

Ultimately, financial discipline empowers us to make choices that align with our values and aspirations. As we continue our journey, let us embrace the lessons learned and strive for a future where financial wisdom is passed down through generations, creating a legacy of prosperity.

By saving and spending wisely, you'll develop a healthier relationship with money, free yourself from financial anxiety, and empower your future. Whether saving for a dream home, preparing for retirement, or simply ensuring that your daily expenses are covered, money boxes can guide you toward a more fulfilling, financially secure life.

This realization highlights how financial discipline can lead to a cycle of generosity. By saving, we create opportunities for ourselves and others, fostering community and connection.

As we wrap up this chapter, I encourage you to reflect on your relationship with money. How do you view saving? Is it a burden, or is it an empowering practice?

In This Chapter...

We explored how the journey of financial discipline is not always easy, but the rewards are profound. By implementing the box system, prioritizing savings, and adopting a mindset of abundance, you can transform your financial landscape.

Remember that it's not just about the money; it's about the freedom and opportunities that come with it. As you embrace this journey, consider the impact you can have on yourself and those around you.

So, let's start saving and watch our financial fortresses grow. The adventure of financial discipline is waiting for you—embrace it and discover the profound possibilities that lie ahead.

₹6
BECOMING YOUR OWN BANK

FAQ

Q: How do you encourage your family to save?

I'm lucky—both my wife and son have developed saving habits that often outshine my own! But for others who are trying to inspire family to save, here's a simple trick: if someone asks you to spend on something, ask them to save for it in a specific "box" until it's full. It's a psychological approach—once they see that goal taking shape, they'll spend more cautiously.

"Do not save what is left after spending but spend what is left after saving."

- Warren Buffet, Philanthropist

Imagine having the power to fund your own dreams and navigate emergencies without relying on banks or loans. Picture a future where you control your financial destiny, are free from debt, and can make decisions on your terms. This is the essence of "becoming your own bank"—a strategy that grants you financial freedom and peace of mind.

Self-financing is about using your own resources to cover expected and unexpected expenses rather than turning to external loans. It frees you from high-interest payments, offers greater control over your financial choices, and brings mental clarity by eliminating debt stress. Without loan commitments, you're able to make financial decisions that align with your values, and your money stays with you instead of being lost to interest and fees.

This chapter explores the benefits of self-financing and reducing dependency on loans. By building and managing your own emergency fund and savings, you can achieve financial security and reduce stress from debt.

As I've mentioned multiple times before, self-financing is a strategy where you rely on your own resources instead of borrowing from external sources like banks or creditors. While this approach doesn't provide instant results, it offers long-term benefits, such as avoiding high-interest payments, gaining full control over your finances, and alleviating the emotional burden that often comes with debt. For instance, if you anticipate needing ₹1 lakh in six months, self-financing allows you to save ₹20,000 each month. By the end of the six months, you will have the full amount needed without borrowing.

One of the primary advantages of self-financing is that it removes the stress of repaying loans.

When you minimize your dependency on loans, your overall financial health improves significantly. Loans may seem like a quick fix, but they come with costs—often in the form of high-interest rates, repayment obligations, and the risk of long-term debt accumulation. Reducing or eliminating the need for loans frees up your income for more productive uses, whether it's investing, saving for the future, or covering immediate expenses without added stress.

For example, consider my neighbor, Sunita Aunty (name changed). Now about 60 years old, she used to rely heavily on loans for unexpected expenses. One day, about 9-10 years ago, I saw her sitting in distress, holding her head. I asked what was wrong, and she shared that her sons had stopped providing financial support, and all she had was her husband's pension. When her health started to decline, she had to take out a loan to cover medical expenses. As I had done with others, I explained the concept of self-financing to Sunita Aunty.

By adopting this approach, she began building an emergency fund using her pension. Over time, she no longer needed to take out loans for unexpected expenses like medical bills, car repairs, or family emergencies. Instead, she was able to draw from her own savings, improving her cash flow and avoiding the financial strain of loan repayments. This shift not only improved her financial health but also her mental well-being, as she felt more in control of her money and her future.

Self-Financing as a Long-Term Strategy

It's important to remember that self-financing is not something that happens overnight. It's a financial mindset that requires consistent effort to save, manage, and plan for the future. The key is to anticipate your future needs and begin financing them from the moment you set those goals.

This approach can be applied to both small and large financial goals. Whether you're saving for an emergency fund, a big-ticket purchase, or retirement, the principle remains the same— consistent, disciplined saving. By planning ahead, you ensure that you'll have the funds available when you need them without having to turn to loans or credit. Self-financing is all about creating a secure financial future for yourself by taking control of your savings and planning ahead. By reducing your dependency on loans, you not only improve your financial health but also gain greater peace of mind, knowing that your future is in your own hands.

Benefits of Self-Financing

Self-financing doesn't just improve your financial health—it also offers significant psychological benefits. Knowing that you have a safety net in place reduces anxiety and stress. Instead of worrying about where the money will come from when an emergency arises, you can handle it with confidence. You've already planned for it, and that peace of mind is invaluable.

When you're not burdened by debt, your mental well-being improves. You feel more in control of your life, which boosts your confidence and enables you to make better financial decisions. This empowerment leads to healthier financial habits and greater long-term stability.

How Does Self-Financing Help?

Self-financing helps in two crucial ways:

Financial Health:
Transitioning from depending on loans to self-financing can dramatically improve both your financial and psychological well-being. Here's how:

When you rely on loans or borrowing to cover expenses, you're constantly playing catch-up. You're not just paying off the original loan amount; you're also dealing with interest, which adds a financial burden that can compound over time. This situation can strain your finances, limiting your ability to save or invest for future goals.

In contrast, when you create your own emergency fund and practice self-financing, you proactively manage your money. You're setting aside funds in advance for planned or unforeseen expenses. This eliminates the need to borrow and, in turn, helps you avoid the stress that comes with debt repayments. Having that financial cushion means you can cover unexpected costs without panicking or scrambling for loans.

This shift to self-reliance improves your overall financial health because you're no longer losing money to interest payments or being weighed down by repayment deadlines.

Moreover, planning for your financial needs ahead of time gives you a greater sense of control. When you're in charge of your finances, you have more freedom to make decisions that align with your priorities. You can focus on building wealth rather than constantly recovering from debt.

By avoiding loans, you free up your income for savings and investments, improving your long-term financial outlook. You're not losing money to interest or drowning in repayment schedules. Instead, you're building wealth for the future.

Psychological Health:
Having a financial safety net significantly reduces stress and anxiety. When you're prepared for unexpected expenses, you feel secure knowing that your future is in your hands. By planning ahead, saving consistently, and creating your own "bank," you can achieve both financial freedom and mental peace. The long-term benefits far outweigh any short-term sacrifices.

Relying on loans and credit can create a vicious cycle that undermines both financial and personal well-being. The allure of quick access to funds—whether for wants or needs—can quickly spiral into a situation where a significant portion of your income goes towards loan repayments, leaving little room for savings or financial growth.

Understanding the Loan Impact

It's crucial to understand that not all loans are inherently bad. Loans for necessary, well-planned investments—such as buying a home or funding education—can be smart financial moves if managed correctly. However, problems arise when loans exceed your income or are taken for non-essential purposes. In such cases, they can become burdensome and jeopardize your financial health.

Loans not only affect your bank account but also take a mental toll. The constant pressure of repayments can cause stress, leading to anxiety and a feeling of financial insecurity. This emotional burden can spill over into other aspects of life, affecting relationships, workplace performance, and overall quality of life.

The key is to avoid unnecessary loans, plan carefully for the necessary ones, and keep debt under control. By reducing your reliance on credit, you gain more control over your finances and, with it, more peace of mind.

The Role of "Money Boxes" in Loan Management

This all ties back to the importance of having your financial "money boxes" well-structured and planned in advance. When boxes—such as your savings, emergency funds, and loan repayment funds—aren't well-defined or properly managed, financial chaos can unfold.

Importance of Planning Your Loan Box

One of the key issues is not having a "loan box" in place when a loan becomes necessary. This is where many people falter—whether it's for a house, a car, or any other major purchase. If that box isn't ready, meaning you haven't set aside money specifically for handling loan repayments or factoring in how the loan fits into your overall financial picture, you'll likely face problems.

The key question to ask is: was that loan even necessary? For instance, a loan for a house may be essential, but a loan for a luxury car could be a poor financial decision, especially if it disrupts your current lifestyle. No loan, no matter the purpose, should ever drag you down to the point of disrupting your daily life.

Main Drawbacks of Relying on Loans

1. **Constant Debt Cycle:** Once you start taking out loans or using credit, especially for non-essential purchases, it becomes

easy to rely on borrowed money for every financial need. The monthly repayment burden can strain your budget, pushing you into a perpetual debt cycle. If you're only paying off interest and barely reducing the principal, it can feel like you're making no progress in clearing the debt.

2. **Interest Accumulation:** One of the biggest issues with loans is interest. Interest payments add up over time, making your original debt much more expensive than it was initially. For example, if you take out a loan to buy a car or an unnecessary luxury item, you end up paying much more than the original value of the item due to high interest rates.

3. **Disruption of Financial Stability:** When loan repayments take up a large portion of your salary, your ability to plan and allocate funds for other essential areas of your life diminishes. Instead of focusing on savings, investments, or even daily expenses, much of your income is spent clearing debt. This constant cycle can quickly destabilize your financial health and threaten your long-term financial security.

4. **Stress and Anxiety:** The strain of managing loan repayments can have a serious impact on your mental health. Constantly worrying about how to make payments can lead to stress, which affects not just you but also your relationships with family and loved ones. The pressure of managing both loan payments and everyday expenses creates tension, potentially leading to disagreements and discord with those closest to you.

5. **Compromising Future Goals:** Taking out large loans for wants (rather than needs) can hinder your ability to achieve long-term financial goals such as buying a home, funding your children's education, or saving for retirement. Instead of working toward these milestones, you find yourself trapped in a cycle of repayment and accumulating interest, which compromises your future plans.

Strategies to Minimize Loan Dependency

1. **Prioritize Needs Over Wants:** Many people fall into the trap of taking out loans for luxury items, such as expensive cars or vacations. One of the most effective strategies to reduce loan dependency is to clearly separate wants from needs. If the

expense isn't a critical need, avoid borrowing money to cover it.

2. **Pre-plan for Major Expenses:** If you know you'll need a large sum of money for a future purchase, like a home or vehicle, start saving now. Create a financial plan where you consistently allocate a portion of your income toward this goal. This proactive approach can minimize the amount you need to borrow and shorten your repayment period.

3. **Limit the Loan-to-Income Ratio:** Before taking out any loan, ensure that the monthly payment doesn't exceed a manageable percentage of your monthly income. A good rule of thumb is that your loan repayments (for non-essential items) should not exceed 30-40% of your take-home pay. This ensures you still have enough left for savings and daily living expenses without compromising your financial stability.

4. **Focus on Building an Emergency Fund:** Rather than turning to loans for every financial emergency, create a robust emergency fund that covers at least 6-12 months of living expenses. With this safety net in place, you can avoid taking out loans in times of need, giving you peace of mind when unexpected costs arise.

5. **Plan for Big Purchases, Not Impulse Spending:** Many people resort to loans on impulse to satisfy desires for immediate gratification. By planning for major purchases in advance, you prevent yourself from relying on credit for things that aren't essential. For example, if you want a new car or to make a major home improvement, make it a savings goal instead of relying on instant credit.

Lifestyle Impact:

If your regular lifestyle is being disrupted by the burden of loan repayments, it's a sign that you didn't prepare adequately. If the money box you've set aside for your loan is incomplete or nonexistent, it will inevitably lead to stress. The financial strain affects not just your wallet but also your mental and emotional well-being, leading to issues in other areas of life—whether at home, at work, or even affecting your health.

The Ripple Effect of Financial Stress

As we've discussed earlier, people often fail to realize the full extent of their financial missteps until they find themselves caught in a web of financial stress. Once you're constantly stressed about loan repayments, the anxiety starts to affect all aspects of life—relationships, work, and overall quality of life. This stress creates a ripple effect that touches everything you do.

The psychological burden of loans—especially when not properly planned—can be overwhelming. If someone is financially unprepared and takes on a loan, the mental toll can be profound. Constantly worrying about how to meet loan repayments impacts your sleep, heightens anxiety, and escalates stress levels in your day-to-day life.

But, if you've planned properly—if your money boxes are organized and ready for a loan—it changes everything. Suddenly, you have peace of mind. You know your finances are in control, and the loan becomes manageable. This is where the power of self-financing and having a well-organized financial plan really shines.

The Advantage of Planning Ahead

I've shared before the example of my own travel plans for 2016. I began preparing for that trip back in 2014-15, saving up and aligning my finances so that when the time came, I didn't have to worry about whether I could afford it. I enjoyed the trip fully, and when I returned, I easily transitioned back into my regular life, financially unburdened.

This kind of planning can apply to everything, including loans. If people take the time to plan their finances well in advance and have their savings boxes in place, they will never need to struggle or suffer the consequences of unplanned expenses or loans.

The real benefit of self-financing is the psychological security it provides. With a solid financial plan, you sleep better, feel less stressed, and

know that even if something goes wrong—whether in your business, personal life, or elsewhere—you have a financial cushion to fall back on.

The Wake-Up Call of Unexpected Crises

The impact of the COVID-19 pandemic was a wake-up call for many. People who hadn't planned for emergencies or savings found themselves in dire financial situations, scrambling to survive. In contrast, those who had saved and planned ahead, particularly in middle and upper-middle-class families, were able to weather the storm.

This scenario is particularly true for people who don't think they'll need an emergency fund—until the unexpected happens. Having the foresight to prepare financially allows you to navigate tough times without falling apart.

The Psychology of Spending

One of the most important aspects of managing your finances is to ask the right questions before making any financial decision:

- Why am I spending this money?
- Is it truly necessary, or can it wait?
- Will this expense add long-term value to my life, or is it just a temporary desire?

These questions serve as a filter for your spending habits. Without intentional planning and clear thinking, it's easy to fall into impulsive spending or borrowing, which can lead to a cycle of financial instability and stress.

By sticking to self-financing principles and carefully managing your finances, you'll protect both your financial health and your mental well-being. Proper planning not only creates a solid financial foundation but also cultivates a mindset of control and peace.

Empowering Financial Collaboration

What I'm describing is a practical and insightful approach to managing household finances, especially in middle-class and upper-middle-class families. By empowering both partners to manage money collaboratively, you can create a balance that fosters financial stability and leads to a more harmonious home life. Let's dive deeper into these principles and explore how they can help you achieve a secure, stress-free financial future.

1. Combining Financial Planning with Household Management

Managing a household is akin to managing a business. It requires planning, discipline, and attention to detail. In a traditional household, where one partner is the primary breadwinner and the other manages the home, the homemaker often has a unique perspective on the day-to-day expenses. They know the intricacies—how much food costs, where to cut corners, and where savings can be made. This makes them naturally suited to handle the family's immediate finances.

The breadwinner, on the other hand, typically has a better understanding of external expenses—bills, investments, and larger purchases. By dividing financial responsibilities, each partner can focus on their areas of strength. This collaboration leads to more effective saving strategies and ensures that money is managed thoughtfully. The division of roles, where each person is responsible for specific expenses—whether household or personal—creates clarity. The homemaker ensures essentials are covered while the breadwinner manages larger items like bills or significant purchases.

2. Empowering Women in Financial Management

Empowering the homemaker by providing them with a little extra money encouraging them to save it for their own security, is an essential aspect of financial independence for the household. This ensures that neither partner feels financially dependent. Women, particularly in Indian households, often excel at managing household expenses. Their mindfulness of small savings—such as negotiating better deals or seeking out free items—can lead to significant savings over time. Allowing women to manage a portion of the household finances gives them a sense of empowerment and ownership.

By giving them an additional 10% to save each month, it gradually builds a reserve that acts as a safety net for emergencies or future expenses. This practice not only supports the family's financial security but also fosters trust and partnership in marriage. When your partner feels financially secure, it reduces stress and benefits the entire family dynamic.

3. Breaking Down Gender Stereotypes in Money Management

Traditionally, men have been responsible for managing household finances, while women handle day-to-day household duties. However, encouraging women to take a more active role in financial management can help break these traditional stereotypes. It's often true that women are better savers, thanks to their attention to detail. Small actions, like negotiating for free extras, can lead to significant long-term savings.

Involving women in financial decision-making promotes equality and partnership. This approach eliminates ego clashes and fosters mutual respect. When both partners are involved in planning and saving, there's less friction, and they are more aligned on shared financial goals.

In dual-income households, it's common for both partners to develop independent mindsets, which can sometimes cause friction in how money is managed. Women, in particular, may feel less inclined to contribute to household expenses in the same way men do once they become financially independent. While this isn't always the case, it can happen.

When couples acknowledge these dynamics, they can work together to create a fair and balanced financial system. Both partners should contribute to household expenses, savings, and personal expenditures in a manner that aligns with their specific situation. Open discussions about contributions and priorities can help eliminate friction and ensure financial stability for the family.

4. Avoiding Ego and Encouraging Discipline

One critical issue in many households, particularly where a man is the sole or primary earner, is the role of ego when it comes to managing finances. This dynamic can lead to an imbalance, where one partner feels they must constantly ask for money, even for the most basic needs. By sharing financial responsibilities and empowering both partners to take charge of their financial situation, the ego is kept in check. This not only promotes better communication but also fosters cooperation and mutual respect.

Moreover, it's not just about giving money—it's about teaching discipline. When a partner is given additional funds to manage, they also learn the importance of budgeting, saving, and managing money effectively. Both partners then become more responsible and disciplined with their spending habits, which can have long-term positive effects on their financial security.

In dual-income households, the financial dynamic shifts, especially with more income coming in. While this can increase convenience and provide opportunities to spend, it often leads to higher expenditures as well, such as dining out more often, hiring domestic help, or purchasing luxury items. The key to maintaining financial discipline in such households is clear communication. Both partners should sit down together and agree on how much each will contribute toward joint expenses, savings, and personal expenditures. By doing so, they can save effectively, if not more so than in single-income households.

However, a potential challenge in dual-income households is the tendency to increase spending when more money comes in. The pressure to maintain a certain lifestyle, particularly in corporate environments where comparisons with colleagues are common, can erode savings. Women, in particular, may feel the pressure to spend more on appearances or lifestyle to match their peers. The solution lies in self-awareness and discipline. When both partners take responsibility for their spending and prioritize savings, they can maintain a comfortable standard of living without falling into financial traps.

5.   Planning Personal Expenses for Both Partners

Balancing personal expenses is another essential aspect of financial management. Whether it's for clubbing, dining out, shopping for clothes, or makeup, it's important that each partner has a personal budget. Setting aside a fixed amount for these activities ensures that the household's overall financial plan remains intact. When both partners have predetermined personal expenses, they can enjoy their discretionary spending without guilt, knowing it won't impact the family's essential finances.

By clearly defining what counts as personal expenses and what is allocated for joint or family expenses, both partners have a better understanding of their spending limits. This clarity prevents financial stress and helps each partner maintain their lifestyle without undermining the overall financial well-being of the household.

6.   Planning Ahead for Financial Stability

One of the most important lessons from this approach is the power of planning ahead. Whether it's setting aside extra money for emergencies, planning for an upcoming trip, or saving for a big purchase, preparation is crucial. If every family adopts this mindset—dividing their needs from their wants, creating contingency funds, and ensuring both partners contribute to managing finances—they are much more likely to avoid falling into financial traps. Planning ahead lays a solid foundation for long-term financial stability and peace of mind, helping each partner stay aligned with their goals and make informed decisions.

7.   Involving the Whole Family in Financial Discussions

An important step towards financial security is involving the entire family in discussions about money. Teaching children the value of money at an early age is one of the most impactful ways to set them up for future financial independence. For example, giving kids a fixed pocket allowance with the expectation that they manage it responsibly instills financial responsibility. This practice not only helps them develop money-management skills but also fosters a family culture where transparency and planning around finances are normalized.

When you give your partner more financial freedom, share responsibilities, and plan personal and family expenses in advance, you set a great example for others. Removing ego, encouraging discipline, and empowering both partners can create a financially secure and balanced household. These small steps, though seemingly simple, add up over time, ensuring that both you and your family are well-prepared for whatever life brings.

The Envelope System for Managing Finances

One practical, deeply personal method I use for managing money is the envelope system. This system is simple and doesn't rely on complex apps or digital tools. The idea is to physically compartmentalize funds by placing them in envelopes or boxes, each labeled for a specific purpose. This method helps me track savings, stay focused on financial goals, and avoid tapping into funds designated for future needs. Here's how it works: Every time I receive my income, I immediately divide it into different envelopes for various purposes. One envelope is for household expenses, another for household help salaries, one for savings, and another for emergencies. This system is effective because it keeps finances organized and ensures that every rupee is allocated. I physically write down the purpose of each envelope, making it real. Once money is placed into an envelope, it stays there until the time comes to use it. This method helps prevent unplanned spending and gives me a sense of control over my finances.

Monthly Bank Reconciliation Statement (BRS)

At the beginning of each month, my partner and I sit down to create a Bank Reconciliation Statement (BRS). This ritual helps us review our total income, planned expenses, and any extra funds. It's a structured way to ensure that all expenses—bills, household costs, etc.—are accounted for before we decide to save or spend anything else. This monthly review has been key to maintaining financial clarity and reducing stress about money.

Compounding and Rotating Interest

When managing finances for my family—my parents and brother included—I also use a strategy of rotating interest from investments. By reinvesting the interest earned from investments and not touching the principal, we allow our family's wealth to grow steadily. This approach of compounding interest has shown me the long-term benefits of disciplined and strategic saving.

Saving for Future Needs

Another part of my system involves creating envelopes or boxes specifically designated for future needs. Whether for emergencies or planned purchases, I regularly set aside money in these compartments and only open them when the time is right. At the end of a year, opening these envelopes and seeing how much has accumulated is incredibly rewarding. This system makes saving a habit rather than a chore and gives me a sense of fulfillment.

While this method is simple, its effectiveness lies in its tangibility. Each envelope or box reminds me of the importance of respecting my financial goals and planning for future needs. This system provides a sense of control that no digital tool has ever given me, offering peace of mind in my financial journey.

The Importance of Talking About Money

In many households, discussing finances is avoided, even though it's essential for a healthy financial life. Topics like savings, earnings, or financial management are rarely talked about openly within families—whether it's with kids, spouses, or parents. This silence can lead to misunderstandings and missed opportunities for better financial planning.

For example, when I meet someone close, one of the first questions I ask is, "How much do you make? And how much do you save?" These may seem like basic questions, but they're crucial. The key message here is that talking about money is vital. Money, in itself, isn't about being rich—it's a tool for managing your lifestyle. It can either build your life or cause it to fall apart. The way you manage money is an art, not just about spending for the sake of it.

When you walk through a mall and see something you like, pause and ask yourself: *Do I really need this, or is it just a want?* Reason it out. Often, 'wants' outnumber 'needs,' and that's where many people get into trouble.

Take my friend, for example. He's in the jewelry business and earns well, but his lifestyle is one of extreme spending. His kids wear the latest luxury brands like Louis Vuitton, Gucci, and other designer labels. Everything they own is expensive and top-of-the-line.

On the other hand, my wife and I have raised our son with a different approach. From the time he was around 5 or 6 years old, we taught him the importance of financial responsibility. Now, at 18, he is so practical about money that he often stops me from making unnecessary purchases, saying, "Papa, why waste money?"

Looking ahead, 10 years from now, the person who manages money wisely will be in a much better financial position. In contrast, someone who spends without planning may find themselves stuck, unable to move forward financially.

The Art of Financial Discipline

This book isn't about complex strategies. It's about simple, practical steps that can improve your financial habits. For instance, I don't rely on external tools or subscriptions to manage my money. Instead, I use the envelope system—a method where I allocate money into labeled envelopes for specific needs and goals. Once money is set aside for a particular purpose, I don't touch it until the time comes to use it.

When my family and I travel abroad, we set a strict shopping budget. If something exceeds that budget, we don't buy it. We stick to our plan and manage our funds responsibly. This simple habit has made a significant difference in how we manage our finances.

Practical Advice and Tools

One of the key takeaways from this chapter is that earnings don't define your wealth—it's how well you manage it. It's not about how much you make but how wisely you save, spend, and invest. Effective money management is the key to building financial security and long-term wealth.

The methods I've discussed in this book are simple but effective. Once you understand how to control your spending, the rest falls into place. People tend to spend more when money is visible. By organizing it into envelopes or packets for specific purposes, I can control that impulse. When I see money labeled for a particular goal, I am less likely to spend it impulsively on something else.

This book is designed to equip my readers with the tools to manage their money better, even if they've previously avoided discussing finances. For many, talking about money can feel like an ego issue, but presenting this information in a clear, non-judgmental way creates a safe space for reflection. The goal is to encourage a conversation about money, helping people examine their financial behaviors and how they can improve them.

This book is not a one-size-fits-all solution. Everyone's situation is unique, and advice should be tailored to each individual's circumstances. However, it does serve as a conversation starter, providing practical steps to improve financial well-being and reduce stress.

The key points covered in this book emphasize the importance of simple habits, the necessity of talking about money openly, and the impact of disciplined financial management. If you'd like to make adjustments to any part of it, feel free to let me know!

While loans may seem like an easy solution, they often lead to financial strain. Borrowing comes with a price—high interest rates, long repayment plans, and a loss of control over your finances. By building a strong savings foundation, you can reduce your reliance on loans, avoid the debt cycle, and regain control of your income.

Strategic budgeting, prioritizing expenses, and avoiding impulse purchases are essential steps in breaking free from loan dependency.

The first step toward becoming your own bank is creating an emergency fund. This fund will act as your financial safety net, providing security in the case of unexpected expenses. Start by setting a savings goal—experts recommend saving enough to cover three to six months of living expenses. Decide where to store this fund—consider high-yield savings accounts or other low-risk options that allow easy access when needed. Finally, make regular contributions to your emergency fund, treating it like a non-negotiable expense.

Beyond the tangible financial benefits, there are significant psychological advantages to self-banking. Financial security reduces stress, fosters a sense of control, and promotes mental well-being. Research shows that individuals with robust savings are less anxious and more resilient when facing financial challenges. By building your own bank, you're not just safeguarding your finances—you're also protecting your mental health.

In this Chapter...

We explored how becoming your own bank requires practical steps like setting a budget, tracking your expenses, and prioritizing saving. Start by creating a clear picture of your income and expenses, ensuring you allocate a portion of your earnings toward savings. Explore low-risk investment options to grow your savings over time and develop a disciplined approach to financial management. These steps will get you closer to financial independence, where you can rely on yourself instead of external financiers.

Practical Steps to Take Charge of Your Financial Future:

1. **Plan and save for future expenses** by setting aside designated funds in envelopes or packets for different goals.

2. **Maintain a detailed record of income and expenditures,** possibly through a balance sheet or a bank reconciliation statement, to track and manage your financial activity.

3. **Involve partners or family members** in financial planning and decision-making, ensuring that everyone shares responsibility and understands the financial goals.

4. **Build an emergency fund** by allocating a portion of income towards savings. Aim for at least three to six months of living expenses to cover unexpected costs.

5. **Evaluate the necessity of loans** and ensure that loan repayments do not exceed a manageable portion of your income. Always assess whether a loan is absolutely necessary and if it aligns with your long-term financial goals.

6. **Prioritize expenses** and avoid impulsive purchases to reduce the need for and dependency on loans. Recognize the difference between needs and wants and plan accordingly.

7. **Foster open communication about finances** within families to promote a sense of security and shared responsibility. This creates a healthier, more informed financial environment for everyone.

Now is the time to take charge of your financial future. Start building your own emergency fund today. Set a savings goal, commit to regular contributions, and take control of your financial destiny.

By becoming your own bank, you're laying the groundwork for financial security and resilience. In the next chapter, we'll explore how to navigate financial setbacks, ensuring that no matter what life throws your way, you're prepared to meet the challenge head-on.

₹7
NAVIGATING FINANCIAL SETBACKS

FAQ

Q: Why is money always so important?

Here's what I tell people: if you're uncertain about the importance of money, try going without it. Stop earning for a while, or tell your friends and family that you're broke. It's a reality check. Money is intertwined with many aspects of life, even relationships. It doesn't define happiness, but it certainly plays a vital role in providing security and freedom.

"A big part of financial freedom is having your heart and mind free from worry about the what-ifs of life."

–Suze Orman, Financial Advisor & Author

Imagine this: you're sailing smoothly on your financial journey when, suddenly, a storm hits. Unexpected expenses, job loss, or a medical emergency can throw you off course. But with the right strategies in place, you can weather any financial storm.

This chapter will guide you through preparing for and bouncing back from financial setbacks. By understanding common challenges and learning resilience, you can keep your finances steady, even in tough times.

Before we dive into the practical strategies for navigating setbacks, it's important to recognize how to prevent them in the first place. For many middle and upper-middle-class individuals, setbacks often arise from poor debt management and a lack of savings planning. One major issue is the pressure to keep up appearances. Living beyond your means doesn't just strain your finances—it can also negatively impact your mental, emotional, and social well-being, causing divides in relationships, families, and professional networks.

Insecurity often drives people to compare themselves to wealthier friends, which can lead to financial strain. Social media amplifies this pressure by showcasing others' lifestyles, sometimes triggering unnecessary spending. However, by focusing on sustainable financial habits, you can break free from these influences and set yourself up for long-term stability.

Understanding and accepting your financial reality is critical for long-term success. I encourage a grounded approach to spending and warn against the "live only once" mentality that justifies reckless financial choices. Instead of indulging in fleeting pleasures or unnecessary expenses, I want to highlight the importance of saving diligently and spending thoughtfully. Financial security is not something that happens overnight but is the result of consistent, wise decisions.

By adopting this mindset, you're better equipped to navigate financial storms and continue steering toward a secure and prosperous future.

Common Financial Setbacks for Upper-Middle-Class Individuals

Upper-middle-class individuals, despite having a steady income, often face significant financial setbacks due to mismanagement or lack of planning. Here are some common challenges they encounter:

1. **Emergency Savings Management:** Many upper-middle-class individuals struggle with maintaining an emergency fund. When unexpected expenses arise, such as medical bills or urgent repairs, the lack of a financial cushion can create stress and result in the need to borrow or deplete savings.

2. **Debt Management:** Effective debt management is crucial. If debt is not handled well, it can accumulate and lead to serious financial strain. High-interest loans, credit card debt, or unnecessary borrowing can erode financial health, making it harder to save or invest.

3. **Savings Allocation:** There's often a lack of structured savings for essential needs like healthcare, retirement, children's education, or housing. If not planned well in advance, these needs can become significant burdens later in life.

4. **Employment Satisfaction and Financial Goals:** Many individuals in jobs find that their work doesn't align with their financial goals. Job satisfaction can be tied directly to income levels, and financial stress increases when salaries don't keep up with rising expenses, especially with inflation.

5. **Spending Habits and Lifestyle Choices:** A common setback is spending beyond one's means to keep up with perceived lifestyle standards. The desire to "keep up with the Joneses" often leads to overspending and insecurity. Constant comparisons to wealthier individuals can result in anxiety, leaving people in financial distress.

6. **Social Media Influence:** Social media often intensifies financial pressures. For example, two friends working in the same company may have different salaries, but one may feel compelled to spend like the higher-paid friend, leading to financial strain. The constant exposure to wealthier lifestyles can lead to unrealistic expectations.

7. **Instant Gratification:** The "YOLO" (You Only Live Once) mentality can encourage impulsive spending for short-term satisfaction. While this mindset may feel good at the moment, it often leads to long-term financial instability.

8. **Smart Financial Choices and Accepting Reality:** One of the most important factors in avoiding setbacks is making realistic financial decisions. Comparing your lifestyle to that of wealthier individuals, such as the children of business magnates, is not helpful. It's crucial to understand your financial limits and stick to a budget that aligns with your income and goals.

Effective Financial Management

Effective financial management involves understanding your personal finances, making smart choices, and maintaining realistic expectations. It's important to remember that money saved is money invested, and financial security relies on wise spending and saving decisions. No one else is responsible for your financial well-being; you must take control and plan accordingly.

In our family, we've built a system where each member manages a set amount of money, and we never exceed that amount without discussing it together. My wife, for example, writes down her monthly expenses in a diary, categorizing everything from groceries to extra spending. This helps us keep track of where our money is going and ensures we stay within our budget. Any additional money is saved for specific purposes, like dining out.

My wife is the key to our budgeting success. She's great at finding deals and ensuring we stick to our planned expenses. For larger purchases, like travel, we create a detailed budget that includes everything—tickets, accommodations, and shopping. By sticking to our predetermined amounts, we avoid overspending and practice discipline. I've noticed that many middle- and upper-middle-class families often overspend simply because they haven't set a clear budget or planned ahead.

The Power of Research and Patience in Financial Decisions

Setting a budget is one of the most effective ways to prevent impulse buying and overspending. For example, when we needed new furniture, I was initially willing to spend around 15 lakhs. However, my wife insisted on doing thorough research, even if it meant spending three months. Instead of purchasing from the first store I liked, we visited 25-30 different stores to find the best quality at a fair price. Eventually, we discovered a vendor in Mumbai who supplied the same quality furniture to stores in Hyderabad but at 25-30% less than what I had initially budgeted. This careful approach saved us a significant amount, and it reinforced the idea that thorough research, even if it takes time, always pays off in the long run.

This habit of researching before making a purchase extends beyond furniture. My father always told me that to understand the true market value of anything, you need to ask at least 10-15 people. Just because an item is expensive doesn't mean it offers the best quality. Patience and research can result in significant savings, and this approach has shaped our family's attitude toward spending.

The Importance of Mindful Spending

My wife, in particular, has a disciplined way of managing even the smallest expenses. She'll evaluate whether buying bread online is cheaper than driving to a store, considering delivery fees, fuel, and time. Even though this might seem minor, she believes that every little bit counts. Her influence has made us more mindful of our spending, both for large and small purchases.

This discipline has also affected our son. He sees how we handle money, and he has naturally adopted a responsible approach to finances. Even though he goes to an international school where many of his peers come from wealthy families, he values money differently. For instance, he prefers to take the train when it's practical, and he thinks critically about his expenses.

What's even more remarkable is his maturity at just 17. He's already thinking about taxes, investment strategies, and how to handle profits from assets. Recently, he even earned a 25-40% return from a stock portfolio I helped him set up, focusing on IT stocks. These are the kinds of conversations we have, and I'm proud to see him developing a genuine interest in managing his finances responsibly.

Teaching Financial Responsibility: A Generational Approach

One day, my son asked me for some money to invest, saying, "Papa, give me some money. I'll do the research, buy some stocks, and make a profit." He even insisted that I take 20% of the profits if he succeeded! I agreed, seeing it as a low-risk way for him to learn. I believe he's on the right path, and it's part of our family's generational approach to understanding money as a valuable tool.

When I write about financial principles, my goal is to show people that managing money well can alleviate much of the stress and frustration in life. Money, when used responsibly, is not just about wealth—it's a tool for stability, good health, and peace of mind. Unfortunately, many people don't realize that financial concerns are often at the root of their anxieties.

The Role of Finances in Relationships

This understanding of money also has a broader societal impact. Finances often influence relationships. For example, when someone seeks a match for their child, the first questions usually revolve around job titles and income. This practical approach reveals how financial security impacts personal relationships. Even when it comes to things like trips, I often find ways to save. For instance, during a trip to Tirupati, I opted for a more thoughtful process rather than just spending extra money on a VVIP pass, saving 10,000 rupees by taking the proper route.

By taking a mindful approach to managing money, we not only secure financial stability but also reduce the stress that often comes with it, leading to a more peaceful and balanced life.

The Power of Persistence and Financial Discipline

At the end of the day, how much effort you put into saving or earning money defines its value in your life. This principle is something I have come to deeply appreciate, and it's the message I want to pass along to others.

One of the best examples I can give is from my own experience. Let me tell you a very real story. Our family was in a joint setup for about 40-45 years, working together in the family construction business. But in 2006, after the passing of one of my uncles, I joined the business with the expectation that everything would continue as usual. However, by 2009, I faced a significant setback with a project abroad in Oman. I had a partner who betrayed me, which left me with no choice but to return to India. That's when I began to see how certain family members were managing finances in ways that were not fair to all of us. After many tense discussions, I made the difficult decision to separate in 2012, both emotionally and financially.

When the split occurred, I was given the responsibility of handling the finances alongside my younger brother. It was a fresh start, but we had no projects and very few resources. It wasn't easy—I even invested in a piece of land that ended up in litigation. But throughout it all, I kept telling myself, "Stay positive. Something will work out." I focused on saving whatever I could and managing expenses carefully, which proved to be crucial during the toughest times.

My breakthrough came in 2013 when I was presented with an opportunity to develop a large project consisting of 343 villas. Initially, I had no funds available, as they were tied up in the litigated land, but I stayed transparent and negotiated with my partner and the landowners. Eventually, I managed to sell a part of the project to raise enough funds to resolve the litigation, buy more land, and move forward. This project became a turning point, and since then, I've continued to grow.

I firmly believe that anyone can recover from setbacks with the right mindset. My advice for staying motivated is simple: always keep some savings, no matter how small. Having savings allows you to remain steady in the face of adversity. Think of money as a tool—when used responsibly, it can help you achieve your goals. Don't misuse it or try to cheat the system because, eventually, things will come full circle. Today, I'm financially successful, and I've even helped those who once caused difficulties for me.

The Ongoing Lessons from Oman

This takes me back to my experience in Oman. I had taken on a small project for the Ministry, but there were challenges I had to navigate. In Oman, you need a local partner to work on construction projects, and I partnered with a local man for this particular project. The agreement was that we would receive funds to build a ministry-level building, with the funds being distributed fairly. But after a couple of months, I realized something wasn't right—the local partner was keeping 70% of the funds and only releasing 30% for the actual construction.

I raised this issue with him, explaining that it wouldn't be possible to move forward with such an imbalanced distribution. Most of the funds were sitting in his bank, and only a small fraction was being used for construction. I had to make tough decisions to ensure that the project stayed on track and to demand transparency from my partner. It was a hard lesson in financial management, but one that ultimately contributed to the growth and success of my business.

This experience taught me the importance of staying vigilant and managing finances carefully, especially in partnerships. The foundation of success in any venture is honesty, transparency, and discipline.

The Importance of Financial Discipline and Accountability

The problem with my situation in Oman was that, as a non-resident, I wasn't authorized to withdraw funds directly, leaving me dependent on my local partner for the release of payments. This created a lot of friction, especially when I realized that my partner was keeping the lion's share of the funds while only releasing a small portion for construction. Despite my efforts to discuss the issue with him, it felt like the situation was becoming increasingly unfair, and my principles were being compromised.

Eventually, I decided to step away from the project. I had another contact in Kerala who offered to manage it, but I chose not to continue under conditions that didn't align with my values. I didn't want to risk the project's success or jeopardize my reputation by working with someone who wasn't transparent. I returned to India, understanding the value of fairness and honesty in business dealings.

That experience taught me a valuable lesson: financial integrity is crucial. If you misuse money or engage in dishonest financial practices, it's bound to backfire. Money should be treated with respect—it can bring about positive results if used properly, but it won't reward dishonesty. This is a principle that I live by in all of my business dealings.

Ricky's Journey: A Lesson in Financial Discipline

This lesson isn't just personal—it resonates with many, including my friend Ricky. I've mentioned his story before, but it's worth revisiting because his journey mirrors many of the same challenges I faced. Ricky initially tried his hand at manufacturing shirts, but it didn't work out. His true passion was photography, so he made the leap and started taking on small projects, charging ₹500 to ₹2000 per job.

Despite the early struggles, Ricky stayed positive and worked hard. Over time, his reputation grew, and he eventually became a well-known photographer, charging premium rates. His Instagram page, @rickendesai, now showcases his talent, and he's been featured in numerous magazines.

Ricky credits the financial advice I gave him, particularly the "boxes" strategy, as a key factor in his success. We would meet up with friends or play poker, and he'd often ask me how I managed my money. I shared my approach to organizing finances, which involved allocating funds into different categories—each box for a specific purpose like savings, investments, and daily expenses. Ricky took that advice seriously, and it made a real difference in his financial journey. He often tells me that staying disciplined with his money has allowed him to grow his business and meet his financial goals.

The Power of Physical Money and Accountability

You may wonder why having money boxes or physically managing cash is so important, especially in today's digital age. Digital savings are convenient, but they often lack the tangible element that can drive discipline and motivation. Physically seeing your money—whether in an envelope, a box, or a savings jar—creates a sense of control and satisfaction that digital savings may not provide.

While digital platforms and apps can certainly help with managing finances, they are not as effective without the internal drive to save. For many people, the act of physically handling or organizing their money can provide a stronger sense of accountability. Personally, I save both digitally and physically, but I find that physically seeing the money pile up strengthens my resolve to continue saving.

I've noticed this myself: when I carry less cash, I spend less. It's similar to how someone trying to quit smoking might leave their cigarettes at home. The nature of money is such that if it's easily accessible and unorganized, it tends to slip away quickly. On the other hand, when money is carefully organized—whether by keeping it in labeled envelopes or neatly bundled—it's much easier to manage and saves you from unnecessary spending.

In essence, the physical aspect of saving—whether it's through cash, gold, or even coins—can create an emotional and psychological connection to the savings process. It's not just about having the money but about feeling in control of it and making intentional decisions about where it goes.

The Importance of Discipline and Purpose in Financial Management

Even in something as simple as organizing your wallet, the way you manage your cash plays a crucial role in staying disciplined with your finances. Personally, I arrange my money by denomination, so I always know exactly how much I have and where it is. I use money clips to keep my cash organized for different purposes—for everyday spending or for other specific needs. This method of organizing helps me stay on top of my finances and avoid unnecessary spending. I even ask friends traveling abroad to bring me new money clips because I enjoy keeping my cash organized this way. It's about discipline, whether it's through your wallet or a broader financial strategy.

At its core, everything ties back to having an emergency fund and building a solid financial safety net. As we've covered in previous chapters, establishing boxes for different financial purposes and becoming your own bank are key elements of financial discipline. Let's now explore a few additional insights on diversifying income and managing finances effectively.

1. Managing and Allocating Funds
Once you've accumulated a fund, it's natural to reassess how you want to use it. Many people start saving with specific goals in mind—such as a vacation or a big purchase—but when they eventually have a substantial amount saved, they might reconsider their plans. They could opt to invest this money instead, turning it into a source of growth rather than just a lump sum for spending.

2. Investment Decisions and Discipline
Over time, saving money teaches financial discipline. For instance, when someone has saved 20-25 lakhs, they're less likely to spend it frivolously. Instead, they might think about investing in

assets like gold, real estate, or stocks. This shift in mindset often leads individuals to seek professional advice from financial advisors, who can help them turn savings into secondary or passive income sources. Investments in stocks or property, for example, can generate rental income, further enhancing financial growth.

3. Shifting from Spending to Saving Mindset

The process of saving money not only teaches discipline but also transforms one's entire approach to finances. As people accumulate larger sums of savings, their spending habits shift. Some may decide to invest in a small business venture, like opening a shop or starting a home kitchen through platforms such as Swiggy or Zomato, especially if they have culinary skills. This transition from spending to saving creates opportunities for additional income and opens new avenues for financial independence.

4. Impact on Family and Long-term Planning

Good financial habits don't just affect the individual—they can have a ripple effect on the entire family. As one partner adopts disciplined saving and investing practices, the spouse often follows suit. Eventually, these habits may be passed down to children, setting them up for long-term financial success. While the journey toward financial stability can be challenging, the rewards—financial growth, security, and peace of mind—are more than worth the effort.

5. Digital Options for Financial Growth

With the rise of technology, there are numerous digital tools available to help individuals track their spending, invest in mutual funds, buy stocks, or automate their savings plans. These digital platforms make it easier than ever to diversify investments and monitor progress in real-time. This ease of access to digital options has democratized wealth-building, allowing anyone to invest and grow their finances, regardless of their starting point.

Looking back at all the experiences and advice shared here, a key takeaway is the importance of aligning financial choices with reality and purpose. In our pursuit of financial success, especially in the upper-middle class, it's easy to get caught up in appearances and comparisons, which can lead us away from our true financial priorities. However, what we often overlook is that true financial security isn't about looking wealthy—it's about being wise and consistent with the resources we have. Financial security comes from making smart, disciplined decisions, sticking to a plan, and living within our means.

This chapter offers practical insights into how to build a strong, secure financial foundation by focusing on disciplined saving, mindful spending, and strategic debt management. Here's a summary of the key principles we discussed:

Key Principles for a Stable Financial Foundation:

1. **Emergency Savings Management**: Having an emergency fund in place is essential to weather unexpected events like job loss, medical emergencies, or urgent home repairs. By setting aside a dedicated portion of your income, you ensure financial stability when unforeseen expenses arise.
2. **Debt Management**: Managing debt responsibly is critical to avoiding financial strain. By staying on top of loan repayments and being mindful of when borrowing is necessary, you can avoid falling into the cycle of debt.
3. **Diversified Savings**: Diversifying your savings across different areas—health, retirement, education, and housing— ensures you're financially prepared for various life stages and challenges. This allows you to focus on long-term financial goals, whether it's for your child's education or securing a comfortable retirement.
4. **Aligning Job Satisfaction with Financial Realities**: Financial well-being is often tied to job satisfaction. Ensure your career choices are aligned with your financial goals. If your job doesn't support your financial aspirations, it's time to reassess.
5. **Breaking the Comparison Cycle**: The urge to "keep up with the Joneses" is a major financial pitfall. Constantly comparing yourself to wealthier peers can lead to unnecessary spending. Instead, focus on your own financial situation and make decisions that align with your values, not external pressures.
6. **Caution with the YOLO Mentality**: The "You Only Live Once" (YOLO) mentality often encourages impulsive

spending. While it's important to enjoy life, wise financial habits are about making thoughtful, future-focused decisions. Financial security doesn't come from instant gratification but from responsible money management.

7. **Teaching Children About Money**: Instilling good financial habits in children prepares them for financial independence. Teaching kids about budgeting, saving, and investing equips them with the tools needed for financial success later in life.

Practical Steps Moving Forward:

- **Evaluate Your Financial Safety Net**: Take stock of your current savings and emergency fund. If necessary, make adjustments to ensure you're covered for unexpected events.
- **Start Building Your Emergency Fund**: If you don't have an emergency fund, start one today. Aim to save at least 3-6 months of living expenses to ensure you're prepared for any financial storms that come your way.
- **Adopt a Disciplined Approach to Money**: Whether through physical cash savings, digital tools, or a combination of both, staying organized and disciplined with your finances is key to achieving long-term stability.

As we move forward, remember that financial security isn't just about accumulating wealth—it's about making mindful choices that align with your goals. By sticking to these principles, you will create a lasting foundation for financial freedom, stability, and peace of mind for yourself and future generations.

₹8
BUILDING A FINANCIALLY HEALTHY RELATIONSHIP

FAQ

Q: How do you handle it if you want something but don't immediately buy it because of your saving habit?

It's all about planning and patience. I save for things in a dedicated "box," and once that box is full, I know I'm ready to purchase. Having a plan and making small sacrifices helps me avoid impulsive buying. It's not deprivation; it's smart preparation.

"I felt like it was time to set up my future, so I set a goal. My goal was independence."

— **Beyonce, Celebrity**

In this chapter, we focus on how to cultivate financial harmony within your relationships, whether with a partner, family, or close friends. We'll look at how money affects relationships and common challenges couples face and provide strategies for managing finances together to ensure a healthy financial future for both partners.

The Impact of Money on Relationships

Money is a powerful force in any relationship, often shaping how we interact with others, how we view ourselves, and how we perceive the world around us. While financial stress is a significant source of tension, the way we manage our finances can either strengthen or weaken the relationships we value most.

- **Financial Transparency:** Open and honest communication about finances builds trust. It's important to be transparent with your partner about income, debt, spending habits, and long-term goals. Keeping financial secrets or hiding purchases can lead to misunderstandings, resentment, and eventually conflict. Establishing an open dialogue about money encourages both partners to work together towards shared financial goals.
- **Spending Habits and Conflict:** Disagreements over money are one of the most common sources of conflict in relationships. Often, these disagreements are not about money itself but about how it is being spent. One partner might prioritize saving and long-term goals, while the other is more focused on living in the moment. Aligning your financial priorities and making sure both partners have a say in decisions can alleviate the stress caused by mismatched spending habits.
- **Money and Social Status:** Money can also impact how we are perceived by others, influencing how we engage in social settings and maintain relationships. The pressure to appear wealthy or successful can drive individuals to spend

more than they can afford, which can lead to stress and even debt. Instead of keeping up appearances, focusing on your own financial health and aligning your spending with your values will create a more stable foundation for personal and social relationships.

Building Financial Harmony with Your Partner

To ensure that finances don't become a source of conflict in your relationship, here are some practical steps to take:

1. **Set Clear Financial Goals Together**: Discuss your individual and joint financial goals, whether saving for a vacation, buying a home, or planning for retirement. Having a common vision and working towards it together strengthens your partnership.
2. **Create a Budget That Works for Both**: Set a budget that allows for both shared expenses and personal indulgences. This helps avoid arguments over money and ensures both partners feel they have control over their finances.
3. **Divide Financial Responsibilities**: Decide who will handle specific aspects of your finances. Whether one person manages the day-to-day expenses and the other handles savings or investments, a clear division of labor reduces confusion and ensures everything is covered.
4. **Emergency Fund and Savings**: Both partners should contribute to an emergency fund and save for long-term goals. A shared safety net ensures both partners feel secure in case of unforeseen circumstances, like medical bills or a job loss.
5. **Plan for Major Expenses**: Before making large purchases, like a car or a home, discuss your options and make sure the decision aligns with both of your financial goals. This will prevent surprises and ensure you're both on the same page.
6. **Respecting Boundaries in Lending**: Avoid lending money to friends or family that could strain your finances or relationships. It's important to set boundaries around borrowing and lending money to prevent conflicts. Offering help without jeopardizing your financial security maintains trust and respect.

Long-Term Financial Planning

Beyond managing the day-to-day, it's important to think about the future—particularly retirement, investment, and insurance. Planning for these long-term needs not only secures your financial future but also ensures peace of mind.

- **Retirement Planning**: Start saving for retirement early. Consider the types of retirement accounts available and choose one that aligns with your goals. The earlier you start, the more time your money has to grow.
- **Investment Strategies**: Diversifying your investments is key to building wealth. Consult with a financial advisor to explore options like stocks, bonds, or mutual funds, and choose investments that match your risk tolerance and time horizon.
- **Insurance**: Life insurance, health insurance, and other coverage types are essential to protecting your financial future and the well-being of your loved ones. Make sure both partners understand the types of insurance they need and ensure adequate coverage.

Financial Independence and the Role of Money in Relationships

Money's role in relationships extends beyond just managing finances—it plays a part in fostering a sense of independence. Financial independence, both individually and as a couple, gives each partner a sense of control and confidence. It allows for personal growth, reduces stress, and creates an atmosphere where both individuals can thrive. This feeling of empowerment and shared responsibility builds a strong foundation for a lasting, harmonious relationship.

Financial harmony is within reach when both partners prioritize open communication, mutual respect, and financial planning. By working together on goals, managing debt, saving wisely, and investing for the future, you can enjoy a stable financial life and a fulfilling relationship. Remember, financial stress doesn't have to be a part of your relationship. By adopting responsible financial practices, you and your loved ones can navigate life's challenges with confidence and peace of mind.

Strategies for Financial Management in Relationships

1. Open Communication:

The foundation of any healthy relationship, whether romantic or familial, is open communication about finances. Discussing income, expenses, financial goals, and even challenges can eliminate misunderstandings and help align expectations. It is essential to have regular financial discussions, especially when it comes to setting joint goals or making major purchases. This transparency fosters trust and helps both partners work toward a common financial vision.

2. Set Realistic Financial Goals Together:

In relationships, it's important to set financial goals that are both realistic and attainable. This means working together to prioritize needs over wants, creating a budget, and ensuring that both partners agree on how to allocate resources. By understanding each other's financial priorities, you can work together to avoid financial strain and maintain a harmonious relationship. A shared vision, such as saving for a house or retirement, ensures both partners are committed to long-term stability.

3. Managing Shared Resources:

In many family structures, particularly in India, there is a shared responsibility for finances, with both partners contributing to the household's financial needs. However, if one partner fails to manage money wisely or isn't contributing adequately, it can create tension. Financial imbalances can lead to resentment over time. It's essential that both partners understand their roles in managing finances, whether it's for day-to-day expenses or long-term goals.

4. Prioritize Financial Education:

Financial literacy is crucial for both partners. Teaching each other about budgeting, saving, and investing and understanding financial products like loans and insurance can empower both individuals to make informed decisions. Educating children about financial responsibility can also be an important step toward creating a financially secure family environment.

The Impact of Money on Relationships

1. Money and Respect:
While money should not define relationships, it often plays a significant role in how people perceive us. Wealth or the appearance of wealth can influence relationships, creating subtle pressures to "keep up" or appear financially successful. This societal pressure can strain relationships, especially if one partner feels compelled to live beyond their means to meet external expectations. The key is to resist these pressures and stay grounded in your financial reality.

2. Financial Stress and Relationships:
Financial mismanagement, overspending, or hidden debt can create stress and tension in relationships. Arguments about money often aren't just about the actual money—it's about the lack of transparency, respect, or mutual understanding. A relationship where finances are managed wisely tends to be more resilient. Financial stability gives both partners the freedom to enjoy life without the constant stress of financial uncertainty.

3. Money and Family Dynamics:
In joint family setups, there can be both support and strain when it comes to finances. Sharing resources is a common practice, but it can lead to misunderstandings if not managed carefully. When multiple people are responsible for the financial health of the family, it is crucial that everyone communicates openly about their expectations and contributions. In such settings, building financial independence for each member while maintaining familial support is key.

Real-Life Examples of Financial Management in Relationships

1. Practical Decisions About Spending:
Managing money well often involves making thoughtful decisions about where to spend and where to save. For instance, when I needed new furniture for our home, I could have easily gone to the high-end showrooms in Hyderabad. However, after doing thorough research and considering alternatives, we found that a wholesale market in Mumbai offered the same quality at a fraction of the price. This decision saved us a significant amount of money and reinforced the importance of making informed, practical spending decisions.

2. Aligning Financial Priorities:
My wife and I have always been on the same page when it comes to budgeting. We've always had regular family meetings to discuss major purchases and shared expenses. For instance, with the furniture purchase, we didn't rush into buying. We discussed our preferences and strategized with the vendor to avoid paying more than necessary. These simple but effective strategies have allowed us to align our financial priorities and avoid unnecessary expenses.

3. Teaching Financial Responsibility to Children:
Financial discipline isn't just about managing money for oneself but about teaching the next generation how to do the same. My son, who is now 18, already shows great interest in managing his finances. He understands the value of saving and budgeting and is even investing in stocks. These values passed down from my own experiences, have shaped his approach to money, making him financially responsible at a young age. This is the long-term impact of wise financial management—it creates a cycle of responsibility that can benefit families for generations.

Money plays a significant role in relationships, and managing it well is essential for maintaining harmony and trust. By engaging in open financial discussions, setting realistic goals, and making informed decisions, couples and families can ensure that their financial future is secure. Financial management is not just about the numbers; it's about creating an environment where both partners feel respected, supported, and empowered. With discipline, transparency, and shared financial goals, you can build a foundation for lasting financial stability and mutual respect in your relationships.

Absolutely, transparency is a foundational aspect of financial harmony in relationships. Without open discussions about income, expenses, and goals, misunderstandings and conflicts are inevitable. Starting from the very beginning with clear, honest conversations ensures that both partners understand the financial landscape. This helps to align expectations and create a sense of shared responsibility. For instance, if a couple knows their collective income and sets a realistic budget for spending and saving, they can better manage their financial resources without unnecessary tension.

Setting Boundaries and Defining Limits

As mentioned, it's important that couples acknowledge their financial limitations and agree to respect them. Financial transparency includes discussing both income and expenses and setting clear boundaries on how much is to be spent on essential needs versus desires. For instance, if a partner makes more than the other, they must both accept this and work together to set priorities that don't create resentment or feelings of inequality. Financial discussions should be about collaboration, not competition. By understanding each other's income and limitations, both partners can make decisions that reflect the family's overall financial health and avoid unnecessary strain.

Social Media's Influence on Spending Habits

The influence of social media cannot be ignored, especially in the age of constant updates showcasing people's extravagant lifestyles. This can lead to feelings of inadequacy or the urge to keep up, even if it strains the budget. It's important to be mindful of these external pressures and to approach them as a family. When one partner sees something they desire, it's crucial to discuss the purchase thoughtfully and openly. The focus should be on practicality and value, not on instant gratification. If it aligns with the budget, then it's a feasible purchase, but if not, exploring affordable alternatives or delaying gratification can help maintain financial balance. Having such discussions openly ensures that financial goals aren't sidetracked by fleeting desires.

Empowering the Partner Managing the Household Finances

To avoid conflicts, it's beneficial to have a system that makes one partner responsible for managing the savings. This can create a sense of ownership and control. For example, the partner who manages savings can have the autonomy to allocate the funds, ensuring they can make informed decisions about where the money goes. In this case, as you mentioned, empowering your wife by giving her the responsibility to manage the savings creates a sense of mutual trust and strengthens the family's financial discipline. Her business mindset further bolsters the family's savings habits, holding both of you accountable. In addition, your son's evolving interest in financial matters showcases the ripple effect of healthy financial practices, setting a positive example for future generations.

Caution in Dual-Income Households

For couples with stable yet limited incomes, especially salaried individuals, a cautious and calculated approach is necessary. Unlike business owners who may take risks in hopes of significant returns, salaried individuals often have fixed incomes, which means there is less flexibility in terms of income and expenditure. It is crucial to work within those boundaries and set realistic financial goals based on the available resources. The focus should be on consistent saving and well-planned investments to build wealth over time rather than chasing quick fixes or unrealistic financial goals. This is where financial discipline comes into play, ensuring that short-term desires don't derail long-term plans

Planning and Categorizing Financial Goals

One way to manage shared financial responsibilities is by putting everything on paper. Categorize expenses and goals into essentials, wants, and desires. With this approach, both partners can work together to prioritize spending and saving for larger goals like purchasing a home, retirement, or higher education. Creating this clear structure helps manage finances in an organized manner, avoiding unnecessary debt and providing peace of mind. A well-organized financial plan can lead to better financial outcomes without the stress of haphazard spending.

The Power of Pooling Resources in Dual-Income Households

In dual-income households, particularly when there is a noticeable earnings difference, pooling the income together is a smart approach. Instead of dividing expenses by income percentage, combining resources allows both partners to work as a team. For example, if one partner earns ₹100,000 and the other ₹200,000, rather than keeping the finances divided, the combined ₹300,000 should be treated as a single fund. This helps to ensure that all expenses are covered without placing disproportionate financial burdens on one partner. Additionally, it ensures that savings are equally prioritized and aligned with the family's long-term financial goals.

Managing Finances as a Couple: Joint Financial Goals and Home Purchases

Couples planning significant milestones like purchasing a home should ensure that their financial plan is realistic and manageable. A key component is making sure that mortgage or loan payments are comfortably within reach, given the joint income. It's critical to avoid overextending oneself—opting for a mortgage term that balances affordability with the desire for long-term ownership, such as a 15- or 20-year mortgage. Effective long-term financial success occurs when both partners contribute toward the home purchase and remain financially disciplined throughout the loan term. By prioritizing mortgage payments over discretionary spending, couples can keep their financial goals on track.

One of the biggest pitfalls in couples' finances arises when individual earnings become a source of competition or independence. Treating salaries as "yours" and "mine" often introduces an element of division, leading to potential conflicts. Instead, viewing the home purchase as a shared family asset strengthens the bond between partners, reinforcing that the home is not just an individual goal but a collective achievement.

Cultural Values and Family Financial Structures

In many Indian families, a shared approach to finances is the norm. This structure encourages interdependence, where financial habits and responsibilities are passed down from parents to children. Unlike the Western focus on early independence, Indian families often promote a unified financial approach, creating a legacy of financial stability, resilience, and long-term planning. This shared financial structure can be a great asset, ensuring that family goals—such as saving for a home or retirement—are pursued together.

As families evolve, especially in India, from joint to nuclear households, there's an inherent shift in how expenses are distributed. While joint families may share the costs of living more collectively, nuclear families face a higher concentration of expenses. For example, dividing one shared kitchen into five different ones increases overall costs and reduces the potential for cost-sharing. Despite the independence that nuclear families bring, they often face financial burdens that need careful planning to avoid strain.

Financial Transparency and Trust in Joint Families

In a successful joint family setup, financial transparency plays a vital role in maintaining trust and unity. Open communication about incomes, expenditures, and future financial goals prevents misunderstandings and reduces the risk of conflicts. Without transparency, family members may feel that some are contributing more than others, leading to feelings of resentment and division.

A practical way to create financial harmony is by assigning financial roles based on individual strengths. For example, a family member with a talent for budgeting could take on the responsibility of managing the collective funds. This ensures a structured approach to handling finances. However, this strategy requires complete trust and transparency; without these, it becomes difficult to manage finances effectively.

Using financial planning tools such as shared budget templates or visual aids can help families stay organized. These tools provide a structured way of tracking contributions and expenses, allowing for clearer decision-making. Dividing family finances into categories—such as essentials, savings, and discretionary spending—further simplifies the process and helps avoid confusion.

A Unified Approach to Financial Management

The key takeaway is the importance of prioritizing transparency and collective financial planning. When everyone is on the same page about family finances, it fosters trust and strengthens relationships. A unified approach can ensure that financial decisions are made based on shared goals, making it easier for the family to grow and thrive together.

In families where differing financial expectations or backgrounds exist, it's essential to address these differences head-on. When partners come from different financial environments or family structures, their perceptions of money can vary widely. Open discussions about these differences can prevent misunderstandings and help align financial goals. These conversations set the stage for cooperative financial planning, ultimately reducing stress and improving the family's overall financial well-being.

Key Takeaways and Advice for Couples to Avoid or Resolve Financial Conflicts

1. Align Expectations Early:
Couples, whether married or considering marriage, should initiate open conversations about financial values, goals, and boundaries before making long-term commitments. Different spending habits, such as one partner being accustomed to conservative spending and the other to more lavish spending, can lead to conflict. Discussing these differences early on prevents disappointment and resentment later.

2. Shared Financial Vision:
A common cause of financial disagreements in relationships is a lack of a unified financial vision. For example, one partner may prioritize long-term savings for retirement, while the other wants to spend on immediate experiences. To avoid this conflict, couples should create a shared financial plan that incorporates both long-term objectives (e.g., purchasing a house, retirement) and short-term goals (e.g., travel, personal experiences). This ensures that both partners' needs are met while aligning priorities.

3. Compromise and Adaptability:
Navigating financial disagreements requires flexibility and adaptability from both partners. For example, if one partner has been financially supported by their family and is used to spending freely, they may need to adjust when faced with different financial constraints. Both partners must be willing to meet halfway, respecting each other's financial limitations and aspirations to avoid conflict and ensure balance.

4. Encourage Financial Independence:
Couples from different financial backgrounds may benefit from each partner's encouragement of financial independence. This could involve one partner taking on freelance work or additional projects to fund personal goals without burdening joint finances. This helps to maintain a balance between shared responsibilities and personal financial desires, preventing one partner from feeling overwhelmed by the other's expectations.

5. Regular Financial Check-Ins:

Since financial situations can evolve over time, couples should schedule regular check-ins—monthly or quarterly—to revisit their financial goals and adjust as needed. This ensures that both partners stay aligned, address any concerns promptly, and avoid misunderstandings or financial stress.

6. Understand Financial Compatibility:

Before committing to a long-term relationship, it's important for couples to understand each other's approach to finances, including their views on debt, savings, and financial risks. Some individuals are comfortable with taking on debt, while others prefer to avoid it. Recognizing these differences early can help prevent conflicts later on by ensuring both partners are on the same page.

7. Learn from Past Examples:

Reflecting on the experiences of friends or family members who have faced similar financial struggles can provide valuable lessons. Couples can learn about the importance of transparency, compromise, and adaptability. Real-life examples of financial conflict or successful joint financial management can provide useful insights and help couples avoid making the same mistakes.

Open discussions around finances, though challenging, are crucial for fostering trust and mutual understanding in a relationship. Financial harmony is built on clear communication, mutual respect, and a willingness to adapt to each other's needs and circumstances. By following these strategies, couples can strengthen their bond and create a solid foundation for a financially secure future.

Here's a breakdown of how these elements work in practice:

1. **Sacrifice and Compromise**
- **Temporary Sacrifice:** In situations where partners come from differing financial backgrounds—such as one partner from a wealthier family and the other from a more conservative one—compromise often involves temporary sacrifices. The partner accustomed to more spending may have to adjust their lifestyle to accommodate the partner's more frugal habits. This could mean reducing extravagant purchases or delaying major lifestyle upgrades to ensure financial stability for both.

- **Mutual Adjustment:** Over time, if the couple works together to meet their shared financial goals, they may find a middle ground where both partners can eventually fulfill their individual desires. The key is being patient and recognizing that sacrifices made in the short term can lead to greater rewards later.

2. **Transparency and Trust**
- **Clear Communication:** For financial compromise to be successful, there needs to be open and honest communication. Couples need to discuss their goals, limitations, and expectations clearly. If one partner feels like they're always making sacrifices without seeing any benefit in return, it can create resentment. Regular discussions and transparent planning are vital.

- **Family Guidance:** In some cases, particularly in traditional family structures, elders can act as mediators or guides. Parents or older family members can provide valuable advice based on their own experiences, offering insights into how couples can manage their finances without losing sight of their relationship goals.

3. Achieving Balance

- **Gradual Change:** Sometimes, when two people from different financial outlooks come together, it requires a gradual change in habits. A couple may need to go through phases where they make concessions on how they spend or save. Over time, the couple might agree on rules that balance both of their desires—such as allocating a set amount for discretionary spending or deciding on certain goals for savings and investments.

- **Financial Plan Review:** It's also helpful to review financial plans periodically, as priorities might shift over time. Regularly checking in on goals can help both partners feel like they're contributing and moving toward a common vision.

4. Parental or Elder Influence

- In many households, the influence of elders—whether parents or other respected family members—can significantly shape financial decisions. Elders, often possessing more life experience, can offer valuable emotional support and practical advice when it comes to navigating financial disagreements. They may help mediate conflicts, providing balanced perspectives that encourage compromise and unity.

Elders frequently emphasize the importance of financial responsibility and long-term stability. They are often the ones reminding younger couples to prioritize saving and planning for the future rather than succumbing to short-term desires. Their advice is grounded in experience, teaching the value of building a secure financial future, especially as the couple plans for milestones like buying a home, funding education, or preparing for retirement.

Planning the Retirement Boxes

Reflecting on financial management, one of the most critical aspects is planning early for retirement. I've observed many people in their later years struggling due to a lack of retirement planning. In their 30s and 40s, they often prioritize spending on their children's education or their own immediate desires, failing to save adequately for their future. The reality is that without proper preparation, retirement can be an overwhelming and uncertain period.

From personal experience and observing others, I've learned that retirement planning must begin in your 30s or 40s. Even if you start with small contributions, over time, these will accumulate and provide a comfortable cushion. Early saving, even in modest amounts, can make a significant difference in the long term.

As you begin your career, it's important to allocate your income into different "boxes" for various needs and goals. This approach ensures that saving remains a priority even as your lifestyle improves with salary increments. Initially, you may start with insignificant amounts—perhaps saving 10% of your income. As your earnings grow, it's crucial to maintain the habit of saving, even if it means a modest lifestyle upgrade. The idea is to save a portion of every increase in income, even if the amount is small.

For me, the concept of a "retirement box" has been transformative. It's not just about setting aside funds but creating a psychological boundary that keeps the money untouched until retirement. This practice has helped me resist the temptation to dip into the fund for emergencies or non-essential purchases. The "retirement box" ensures that I have a secure financial future, free from the dependency on external support when I am no longer earning regularly.

The key to retirement savings is consistency, not perfection. Don't wait for the "perfect moment" to start saving—begin as soon as you're able. By your mid-30s, aim to save at least 10% of your income, gradually increasing that percentage over time. As you move into your 40s and 50s, this should rise to 25-30%, ensuring that by the time you reach your 60s, you will have built a solid financial cushion for retirement. If you don't start saving early, you could find yourself relying on others or even social security, which can be a difficult and limiting position.

The importance of starting early and building a financial foundation cannot be overstated. The discipline of saving consistently, especially for retirement, can significantly impact your quality of life in the future, providing security and freedom when you no longer have a steady income.

Building Capital Before Investment

Before diving into complex investment options, I always advise people to build their capital first. Without a strong financial foundation, you're essentially gambling with your money. It's like trying to invest without having enough savings to back up your basic needs. By first focusing on building savings and creating a stable income stream, you change your entire mindset. You begin to see investment opportunities not as risks but as ways to grow your wealth. This foundational step makes you more confident and less anxious about immediate survival, allowing you to embrace investment opportunities with a clearer vision.

The Importance of Insurance

Insurance is another non-negotiable aspect of financial planning. While I won't go too deep into the subject, I want to stress that life and medical insurance should be foundational in any financial plan. These two types of insurance provide peace of mind, knowing that if the unexpected happens, your family won't be left in financial turmoil. Whether it's life insurance to protect your loved ones or medical insurance to cover healthcare costs, these should be top priorities. Once you have these in place, you can confidently move forward with other financial goals.

The Impact of COVID-19 on Financial Habits

The COVID-19 pandemic served as a wake-up call for many when it comes to money management. I saw firsthand how it shifted perspectives. For some, it led to increased spending and decreased savings, which caused severe financial strain. The lesson here is simple: financial discipline is paramount, especially in uncertain times. Even if saving doesn't seem urgent when everything feels unpredictable, that discipline ensures you're prepared for whatever life throws at you. The pandemic reminded many of the importance of having a financial cushion to rely on during times of crisis.

Balancing Lifestyle Choices and Financial Stability

A significant challenge I see with many couples and individuals is balancing lifestyle choices with financial stability. It's tempting to upgrade your lifestyle as soon as you hit a milestone, but this should never be done unless you're sure you can sustain it in the long term. Financial stability comes from being realistic about your resources and not allowing momentary desires to derail your financial health. The key is to know your financial picture thoroughly and avoid impulse spending. It's about prioritizing long-term stability over short-term gratification.

Impulse purchases have always been something I've been cautious about. Whenever I consider a potential purchase, I ask myself: "Is this truly necessary? Does it align with my larger financial plan?" More often than not, I find alternative, more economical options that fulfill the same need without straining my resources. By practicing this approach, I've learned to maintain control over my spending and ensure that each purchase is aligned with my broader financial goals.

Being Proactive About Financial Independence

One important lesson I've learned is the significance of being proactive with finances and always moving toward financial independence. It's easy to rely on others—whether parents or children—to help us out in the future, but that's a dangerous path.

I've always believed in the principle of standing on my own two feet financially, regardless of external circumstances. Being self-reliant ensures that I can weather any storm without depending on anyone else for financial support.

My Experience with My Parents' Retirement Boxes

This need for financial independence is particularly important when it comes to retirement planning, which brings me to a personal experience with my parents. I see a recurring issue in India: many elderly people face financial difficulties in their retirement years because they expect their children to take care of them. However, this is a risky assumption. Children may move abroad for better opportunities, or even if they remain locally, their own financial commitments may limit their ability to support their parents. As a result, many elderly individuals face a tough reality when they don't have enough saved for their retirement.

For this reason, I always stress the importance of parents (and couples, in general) taking responsibility for their own retirement. It's about becoming "selfish" in ensuring financial independence for the future. The "retirement box" I often refer to is meant to be untouchable—reserved for when it's truly needed in retirement. This principle isn't just about having money set aside; it's about creating a financial security net that allows you to live freely without being dependent on others for support. It's a crucial lesson and one that, if learned early, can lead to a more secure and dignified future.

Adapting to Changing Desires and Needs with Age

As we age, our desires and priorities evolve. When we're young, the focus is often on showing off, buying trendy items, and experiencing new things. We want to live life to the fullest and keep up with the latest trends. But as we reach our 50s or 60s, that shift in priorities becomes more apparent. We become less interested in impressing others and more focused on our own well-being, health, and security. The desire to keep up with appearances fades, and what's left are the essential needs for peace of mind and financial stability.

This shift is natural, and it's a reminder that saving during the early years of your working life will make this transition smoother. Instead of being concerned about spending on luxury items, you'll be more focused on covering the essentials, like health care, housing, and a comfortable lifestyle, without the need to work continuously.

The Importance of Early Retirement Savings

Saving for retirement isn't just about stashing away money for a rainy day—it's about being proactive in securing your future. With increasing healthcare costs and the rising cost of living, it's essential to be mindful of the future. By starting to save early, even a small percentage of your income in your 30s (around 5%), and gradually increasing it as your income grows, you can ensure that you're prepared for the unexpected expenses that come later in life.

The earlier you start, the more time your money has to grow through compounding interest. If you wait until your late 40s or 50s to think about saving for retirement, you've already missed out on crucial years of growth. And without enough savings, you may find yourself needing to work well into your old age, something most of us want to avoid.

As I always say, "Save money, and money will save you." The key to a secure future is a disciplined approach to saving—putting money away regularly and ensuring it grows over time to meet your needs when you no longer have a regular income.

Retirement Readiness: Planning Ahead

Retirement readiness is about more than just saving money—it's about preparing yourself financially and strategically to live comfortably once your working years are over. A successful retirement plan ensures that you can enjoy your later years without relying on others for financial support. It allows you to live independently and with dignity.

The most effective retirement plans begin early. In your 30s and 40s, you might be focused on building a career or raising a family, and retirement might feel far off. However, starting to save for retirement around age 35 is crucial. These savings should go into an untouchable "retirement box," which is dedicated solely to your future. This is a fund that you don't access until you reach retirement age.

Learning from Personal Experience

Many people fail to plan properly and, as a result, end up relying on their children or other family members when they can no longer work. I've seen this first-hand with my father. Like many in his generation, my father didn't set up a separate retirement fund, relying instead on family support. When the family business was divided in 2012–13, I was entrusted with managing his share of the funds. This responsibility was humbling, and I knew that I needed to ensure my father's financial security without taking unnecessary risks. It was a lesson in how important it is to plan ahead for retirement, both for yourself and for the well-being of those around you.

The process of setting up a structured financial plan for my parents has reinforced my belief in the importance of retirement planning. By starting early, you can ensure that both you and your family are financially prepared for the years ahead, no matter what life throws your way.

Building a retirement fund and establishing a "retirement box" has been a crucial aspect of my financial strategy. By separating funds for specific purposes, especially retirement, I ensured that my parents could live comfortably without the financial worries that often come with aging. This approach wasn't just about setting aside money—it was about managing it responsibly and allowing it to grow over time.

I started by creating a dedicated pool of funds for my parents' retirement. This retirement box was meant to cover their living expenses, healthcare, and leisure activities. The key was to make sure the principal amount was safe, so I invested it in a high-interest account within my company. This way, the fund could grow without depleting the principal. Each month, I send them the interest earned, which provides them with enough income to cover their daily needs and even allows them to enjoy some extra activities, like travel. This arrangement ensures their comfort and peace of mind, and it's deeply rewarding to know that they are financially secure.

Reflecting on this setup, I realize that a structured, disciplined approach to saving is the key to financial freedom, especially during retirement. It's essential to plan for the future, ensuring that your needs will be met without depending on others. Watching my parents live securely, without financial strain, has reinforced the importance of early, consistent saving. In my own life, I've adopted the same approach, setting aside funds in separate savings boxes for various goals, including my own retirement.

The principle of building a solid foundation of savings before making complex investments has been a key learning for me. Investment decisions should come after ensuring that your basic financial needs are met. Whether it's for a home, a car, or a vacation, the goal is to allocate funds systematically—by creating a savings box for each goal and gradually contributing to it. Once the money is saved, you can reassess whether it should be spent on the intended purchase or invested elsewhere, allowing it to work harder for you.

It's all about having a solid financial plan that allows you to navigate your goals, stay disciplined, and make your money work for you. If you can build a consistent savings habit and invest wisely, you'll not only be prepared for retirement but also secure enough to take on new opportunities as they arise.

Building the initial savings capital can be one of the most challenging steps in personal finance. It's not about having a large amount from the outset; it's about creating a foundation that allows for future growth. Think of it like setting a budget for a meal. If you have more money, you have more options, but if you don't have enough to start with, your choices are limited. Money, in this sense, doesn't just provide purchasing power—it shifts your mindset. Once you have some capital, it opens up opportunities and changes your approach to both saving and spending.

But the real challenge lies in making your savings grow. This is where many people falter. They save diligently but either squander their savings on unwise investments or make impulsive spending decisions. Money can bring security and happiness, but only when it's handled with care and intention. This understanding of money as a tool is something my father instilled in me, though his generation had a different approach. They were more conservative in their spending, often due to circumstances that necessitated saving. In contrast, today's world offers more opportunities but also comes with the pressure of constant comparison, especially with social media amplifying lifestyle aspirations.

The middle and upper-middle classes, in particular, face both the potential for financial growth and the temptation to overspend. Managing money effectively isn't just about accumulating wealth—it's about creating a balanced lifestyle that aligns with your financial reality rather than with others' curated lives. I've seen far too many people regret not managing their finances well early on, especially when their income increased, but their spending habits didn't change accordingly.

The post-2020 world has especially shown us the importance of financial discipline. The pandemic revealed how unprepared many people were for unforeseen circumstances. The lockdowns led to pent-up demand for experiences, and many overspent on things like luxury travel or cars, often beyond their means. Without financial discipline, these impulsive purchases destabilized many people's finances. This taught us two key lessons: the importance of preparing for the unexpected and the need for a solid financial plan that accounts for both our desires and the realities of our income.

This balance is crucial—savings shouldn't just be about accumulating money but about creating a cushion that can weather life's storms. It's about preparing for those rainy days and being disciplined enough to resist the temptations that can lead to financial strain. If there's one thing that the pandemic has reinforced, it's that we must prioritize financial security in ways that go beyond instant gratification.

In this Chapter...

To make a really long story short, money management goes beyond investments or insurance policies. It's about making conscious choices with the resources you have. Before making any purchase, I always ask myself if it's necessary. I value what I earn and spend thoughtfully. There was a time when I almost bought a luxury car, but I paused, realizing it wasn't a true need, and instead chose to save for something more essential. This practice of discipline has kept me grounded over the years.

Luxury can be alluring, but it's crucial to maintain balance. Living beyond your means for fleeting pleasures can put your long-term security at risk. I've seen even celebrities who once flaunted their extravagant lifestyles only to find themselves financially struggling. Social pressures amplify this behavior, pushing people to chase status rather than focusing on their own genuine needs.

The solution lies not in comparison but in prioritizing financial health. While insurance is an important safety net, true financial security is built on a solid, lasting foundation.

Managing finances within a relationship requires mutual sacrifice, trust, transparency, and a shared commitment to long-term success. Couples must understand each other's financial habits and adjust expectations to support both the relationship and their collective goals. When these principles are followed, it leads to greater financial stability and a stronger, more resilient partnership.

"THE SECRET TO GETTING AHEAD IS GETTING STARTED."

— *Mark Twain*

EPILOGUE

FAQ

Q: What advice would you give to someone struggling with wants and desires?

It's a challenge, I know, but try using the "box" method in your daily life. Make a list of your needs and wants. Prioritize your needs first and set aside money for those. For wants, create a separate box, and add to it gradually. This way, you won't just fulfill desires on a whim—you'll see your wants materialize through careful saving. In this approach lies the key to winning the money battle.

"Let me give you a tip on a clue to men's characters: the man who damns money has obtained it dishonorably; the man who respects it has earned it. Run for your life from any man who tells you that money is evil. That sentence is the leper's bell of an approaching looter."

— Ayn Rand, Author and Philosopher

As we close this chapter, I want to reiterate some of the most valuable lessons I've learned from saving, managing money, and making conscious decisions about our resources. Saving isn't just about accumulating funds—it's about creating the mental and emotional strength to make wiser choices, prioritize long-term security, and embrace a sense of purpose in how we manage our financial lives.

Here's a brief recap of the principles that saving has instilled in me:

1. **Discipline and Self-Control:** Saving teaches us to delay gratification and prioritize our financial goals over fleeting desires. It's a daily commitment that impacts every aspect of our lives.
2. **Financial Security:** A strong savings habit offers peace of mind, ensuring that when life presents challenges, we have a cushion to rely on.
3. **Goal Achievement:** Every dollar saved is a step toward achieving meaningful goals—whether it's buying a home, securing education, or preparing for retirement.
4. **Understanding Needs vs. Wants:** Saving changes how we perceive spending, helping us differentiate between what we truly need and what is driven by impulse.
5. **Preparedness:** Saving equips us for the unknown, giving us the stability to face life's curveballs with confidence.
6. **Compound Interest Benefits:** Saving early lets us enjoy the power of compound interest, making our money work for us over time.
7. **Reduced Debt:** The more we save, the less we rely on borrowing. This minimizes the stress of debt and interest payments, giving us more freedom to pursue our goals.

Throughout this book, I've shared not just strategies but a mindset that helps guide you toward financial resilience, security, and peace of mind. Remember that the balance between short-term desires and long-term stability is key to financial freedom. While instant gratification may provide temporary satisfaction, sustainable financial growth is built on thoughtful choices and wise investments.

I hope this book serves as a guide to help you shape a financial future that's secure, free of unnecessary worry, and aligned with your true values. Thank you for joining me on this journey—here's to building a future that's rooted in purpose, security, and lasting fulfillment.

ABOUT THE AUTHOR

Anand Mehta, owner and promoter of **Mehta Constructions**, brings over 16 years of expertise in the real estate industry. His strong experience is built on a longstanding partnership with **Modi Properties Pvt. Ltd.**, during which he has successfully executed and delivered more than 1000+ residential homes across Hyderabad.

Anand began his journey in 2005 with the brand **Mehta Constructions**, quickly establishing a solid reputation in the real estate sector. His unwavering commitment to excellence has consistently elevated industry standards, delivering magnificent constructions, refined craftsmanship, and exceptional value for money to clients.

Since its inception, **Mehta Constructions** has been dedicated to construction and real estate development, completing all projects with outstanding quality and within stipulated timelines.

As the **Managing Director and Partner**, Anand oversees key operations for ventures such as **Mehta & Modi Homes, Dilpreet Tubes Pvt. Ltd., Greenwood Heights, Gulmohar Residency**, and **Villa Orchids**. He also serves as a director of **Modi Properties** and is actively involved in its full-time operations.

His vast knowledge and expertise in project execution have propelled the group to achieve remarkable success. Over the years, Anand has focused on creating not just projects but iconic landmarks, striking a balance between cost-effectiveness and world-class quality.

Recognizing the growing maturity of the real estate market and its evolving opportunities, Anand has set new goals, including expanding into **Propproperty** to deliver even greater value to clients.

Partnership with Modi Properties & Investments

- Backed by two decades of experience in the construction industry.
- Proven track record of quality and commitment in residential projects.
- A trusted partner of **Modi Properties**, renowned for excellence and reliability.

www.ingramcontent.com/pod-product-compliance
Lightning Source LLC
Chambersburg PA
CBHW032059080426
42733CB00006B/341